Contents

TESTING THE WATERS

The Elements of Life Series

Book 1 of 4

Most parents and teachers can pick on the warning signs that teens display when something just isn't right. Sadly, this was not the case for Elizabeth. Although her intentions were well and she loved her family, she could not put out the flame that was suddenly ignited upon completing a project for her Freshman-year health class.

"Over the weekend, I took care of my "baby" when it cried. I had been instructed to insert a key into its back to calm it down. This baby simulator put ideas into my head that caring for a baby would be as simple as turning a key. I quickly started to enjoy carrying the baby around with me and pretending that I was a mommy. I wanted to practice, and I wanted my doll to be real."

Elizabeth had an emptiness in her life and could not understand her feelings, and why they were so powerful. She did not express her feelings to her family or community support.

A must-read for parents, teens, professionals, and former teen parents who lived through the real, and shocking deal.
Don't wait for the damage to be done.
Once Elizabeth was successful with her plot, she was reprimanded by her family and the community. Her nineteen-year-old boyfriend, and father of her soon-to-be baby, stayed by her side, but failed to further mature as a support system and father. Law officials did not consider that he was an adult, and having underage sex with a fourteen-year-old girl at the time of her pregnancy. This may have just saved Elizabeth from the suffering and shame that she would further encounter as a young adult.

As a former teen parent, Elizabeth is boldly confessing the truth. She believes that hiding the secret of her pregnancy being intentional will only encourage this matter, which is commonly avoided by society and the media. Elizabeth hopes to encourage other former teen parents to also break their silence in an effort to re-evaluate the statics.

Statistics state that out of 100 teenage pregnancies, 20 are planned. In the teenage brain, the reward system is mainly influenced by friends and peers when it comes to risk-taking.

What would you do if your teens' best friend became pregnant? How would you feel if you discovered that your teen was actually *trying* to get pregnant? What if your teen was dating a person who was encouraging this? What if it was too late?

Mental disorder in teens is also a common problem that goes unnoticed. In an effort to feel better, teens typically self-destruct with reckless behavior and abusing substances such as alcohol and drugs. What are the signs to look for?

By re-living her true experience as a confused teenager wanting to quickly grow up, Elizabeth takes you into her world, and her thoughts which uncover a shocking but real question. Do we really know what is going on in the lives of our children? And what can we do to ensure their emotional and social health?

I encourage you to read on.

"...deeply honest..."

"Elizabeth's book is about a young woman who undergoes the struggles of motherhood and ultimately learns how to navigate the conflicts of life the best way she can. She details various parts of her life that are the cornerstone of teenage life, which include falling in love, school life, disputes with parents, and even life-changing decisions that will not only impact her life but the life of those she loves as well. What Elizabeth has crafted is a great piece of literature that young people and adults alike will find both inspiring and astonishing."

Dominique Jordan
Teen Site Editor at BellaOnline.com
dmnqjrdn@yahoo.com

"Flashback"

"This was an interesting read. Growing up in the same town and reading this is like a little flashback in time. Knowing some of the people & events in this book I wanted to be subjective. The book is well written and keeps your attention. I had almost the same experience as the author and could relate to the story well. The writer is brutally honest and the storyline may seem scandalous to some but in reality is a real life issue. I'm looking forward to reading more."

2busy2stop

"Courage in Spades"

"...I admire Elizabeth's courage first and foremost to tell her story and secondly to do it as in indie e-book publisher. It is fascinating to read the internal dialog of a young woman who makes a conscious decision to prepare to become pregnant and accomplish that mission in a completely pre-meditated way. I am 50 and we didn't talk about teen pregnancy when I was in High School, we whispered about it behind other girls' backs and slut shamed. For Elizabeth to choose to take her story and others like it and be transparent about the motivations and hopes that a pregnancy can seem to "solve" for a young, confused girl who wants to leave home but doesn't have the pragmatism to see beyond senior year, displays a compassion, empathy and honesty we all need at every age and stage of life.

Katie Jane Wennechuk

COPYRIGHT © 2013

E. McNew
Jessie Lang
First Printing December 1, 2013

Fifteen &...What?! The prequel,
Previously Published in August 2013

ISBN-13:
978-1494241308
ISBN-10:
1494241307

Testing the Waters
The Elements of Life Series
Book 1 of 4

Houston TX
Rose-Monet Publishing
Printed in the USA

Disclaimer

This narrative is written to offer information and education to our readers. It is sold/uploaded with the understanding that the publisher and/or author is not engaged to render any type of psychological, legal, or any other kind of professional advice. This content is the sole expression and opinion of the author. Neither the publisher nor the individual author(s) shall be liable for any physical, psychological, emotional, financial, or commercial damages, including, but not limited to, special, incidental, consequential or other damages. Our views and rights are the same: You are responsible for your own choices, actions, and results.

I would like to expressly convey to you (the reader) that if I were to accidentally defame, purge, humiliate and/or hurt someone's person or feelings as a result of reading and/or acting upon any or all of the information and/or advice found in my content, it is entirely unintentional of me to do so.

By continuing to read and interpret the remainder of this novel, *Testing the Waters*, written by Elizabeth McNew, you are waiving any rights to sue in court of law myself and/or any other person involved with this narrative in any way. I, Elizabeth McNew, shall not be held responsible for your ego being shot down or your mental status taking a plunge. If you, the reader, find any of my content to be insulting, malicious, insensitive, or unnecessary, contact me via email @ **mcnewpublishing@gmail.com** so I may rectify the problem.

Acknowledgements

I never would have understood what it truly meant to write a memoir, or any book for that matter, until now. From the emotional rollercoasters, to the sleepless nights, to the constant time-crunches, and sacrificing so much time to spend with my family, this has by far been the most exhausting and rewarding experience of my life.

I want to thank two people who actually believed that I could pull this off right from the start, Ashley and Steele Witchek. If you both hadn't gone out of your way to show your faith in my story, and my ability to tell it well, this book wouldn't be here. You are both amazing people, and I will forever be grateful to have you in my life.

I must thank my Editor, Jessie Lang, who randomly came to my rescue, after the two of us had not made any contact since those awkward pre-puberty days in middle school. Jessie has spent hours shining up this memoir, and she has done it beautifully. Not once has she asked for a thing in return. She has been a mentor and support system in more ways than I could have ever asked. I owe you millions (literally)!

Jeanine Poell and Jessica Cunningham have been like guardian angels, helping me along the way, when I didn't even realize how desperately I needed it. If it weren't for Jeanine, I would have never learned about the important details that every author should know when it comes to publishing (I swear, she's a closet author!). If Jessica hadn't contacted me, I would have completely neglected the importance of a press release and many other critical marketing tactics. You both have restored my faith, in that I still have a hometown that cares, and I can one day return to the lake with confidence and peace, and on a mission to take you both to dinner.

To my friends, who have been on my side for every step of this process, I love you all and I will always remember your kind words. Whether you have financially supported my project or cheered me along the way, you all are a huge part of this!

Haley Rivas (eighteen years strong!), April White (fifteen years!), Devon Seibert (waiting for you...still...) Rebekka Days, Sara Luce-Baxter, Jackie Smith, Brianna Kovach, Kara Botto, Michelle Clarke, Alexandria Brooks, Sara DeLacy-Tegantvoort, Sarah Erb, Molly DeLallo, Tiffany Leathers, Michael Herron, Jeremy Botto, Mark D. Swartz, Ashley Winfrey, Tiffany Jordan, Timber Lee Guymond, Anna Elsie Pacheco, Larissa Christy, Cynthia Bernales (Kindergarten!), Sarah Renee Madden, Lindsey Caven, Nicole Louise Ricioli, Jessalyn Manina, Rachel Campbell, Shanna Benoit, Valerie Santa, Christina Meyer, Sabrina Bouck, Kevin Leonard, Tracina Lefteroff, Ryan Shannon (you've been awesome buddy!), Cathy Beliveau, Jackie Metoyer, Jesica Reaveley, Jesus Mariscal, Megan Johnson (Thanks for your forgiveness ;), Ashley Lucero, Farrah Kuenzi, Kim Real, Tiffany Tworek, Chelsea Sterling, Thomas Lopez, Lorenza Ruby, Luis Estrada, Alyssa Fortune, and the many, many other amazing supporters and friends that I surely have (regretfully) missed.

I also absolutely have to thank my family. Your love, support, and patience have made this possible. My husband has been the most patient, and without his love I would be nowhere. You have revived my spirits and brought life back into my world, and convincing you to marry me will always be the best idea that I ever came up with. Our beautiful baby girl reminds me every day of how special our family is, and how much love and faith you both have given to my daily existence. I love you so very much Steven and Savhanna.

My in-laws are the best that any person could ever ask for. The frequent vacations, weekend mansions, smoky-mountains, busy beach trips, cruises and dinners are only a fraction of why I love you all ;) I feel like I am truly a part of the family, and I have not met any two people that are so giving, humble, normal, accepting, and easy to be around. I love my McNew family to pieces! And of course Grandma McNew and your support, it has been invaluable. Thanks for everything!

My twin sister, Merri. I love you beyond words, like twin style. We have been through the toughest of toughest, and even if it was only myself going through hard times, you were always with me and loving and supporting me regardless of my mistakes. We will always have a bond that only twins can understand and I am lucky to have had you with me literally from day one. You are my best friend merf! I love you!

To my Grandma and Grandpa Curtice, who I will always be living with for seventeen years. You have both given me such beautiful childhood memories. The kind of memories that never leave your heart, and keep you wishing that you could go back to relive them. Through all of my bad choices, struggles, mistakes, and rollercoasters of rock-bottoms, you always treated me with the same compassion and respect as I received as a child. I love you both so very much, words could never describe.

Lastly, to every person who I have known, and have not known, who has ever sent blame and hate my way, before understanding the sad facts, I hope that this story will answer your questions and send a message of compassion and humility.

I have forgiven every single one of you, and I wish you nothing but peace and happiness for the rest of your lives. We all deserve to be free from feelings of hatred and sadness, and by forgiving my "enemies", I have accomplished just that. I hope that you can free yourself and do the same. If you have found this book, I hope that you will absorb this information and end the last line with a sense of hope, forgiveness, and peace.

Dedication

To the pieces of my heart that never stopped beating. I have loved you from day one, I have never stopped, and I always will. My hope is that your questions can find answers and your doubts can find truth. What is meant to exist surely will. The world is a better place because you do.

Without you, this book would not exist. I hold on to the hope that your reading of how you came to exist, will bring an understanding that one day can allow me an opportunity to make things right and finish the important task which was abruptly, unfairly, and suddenly put to an end; which is being your mother; emotionally, physically, and unconditionally. I love you girls, and I wait for the day that this truth brings solace and you can comfortably and freely call me your mom. You have always been my babies, and until my last breath, I will reserve my heart for you infinitely. For now, I hold onto the beautiful and irreplaceable memories that no entity can steal. Down the road, I pray to God every night that I can hold you in my arms and be blessed with even more memories.

To my mom, who has helped me along this road in more ways than I had ever realized until writing this memoir, I wish that I could have thanked you and shown my appreciation much earlier than today, because you definitely deserved my gratitude a long time ago. I am sorry for putting you through so much pain and agonizing years of having to endure the unknown. You have suffered with me, and although this makes me sad, I now understand that I have never been truly alone in this journey. I love you so incredibly much, and I am very grateful for your ability to calmly tolerate my frequent dramatic antics and still love me and understand me all at the same time. I love you mommy.

Introduction

If my life were to unexpectedly end today, there would be no means or way to convey to my precious daughters the permanent place that they have always held in my heart. The unanswered questions and unspoken truth would always remain, and my story would forever be hidden away only to continue as a dark and brutal history. I am letting it go today.

I was inspired to begin writing a memoir after completing an assignment for my Interviewing and Communications college course that I was enrolled in last summer. Currently, at twenty-six years old, I have been hiding myself and my secrets away from society for the last eight years. To sit down and tell a person my full story, which rarely happens, does not do it justice. The many forgotten details and sequences of events, which determined the fate of all involved, can only be recovered through the slow and deliberate process of reliving them while writing this book. After an incredible series of struggles and hardship, from age eighteen to twenty-two, I am ready to come clean to the world and release the truth.

After facing a mother's most horrific nightmare, I was scared that the people in my small hometown of South Lake Tahoe were talking behind my back and putting the blame on me. I eventually developed agoraphobia and suffered from severe panic attacks the moment I would step outside. I did not begin to heal until I made the brave choice of leaving my ex-husband, after re-locating with him to Texas in hopes that the real problem was my location, and the community in it. I was under false hopes.

Another four years of trial and error have gone by, and I now, finally, find myself content. I am in the perfect place to share my story, and reveal the full truth which I have yet to fully disclose to anyone. I am doing this for myself, but also, more importantly, I am doing this for my daughters, my family, and an innocent newborn baby who lost his life with no justice thereafter.

You may be reading this as a friend and supporter of my efforts to create change, you may be reading this as a person who is disgusted by my choices, or you may be reading this as a complete stranger. Regardless of how you may relate to this book, I have one important favor to ask: I ask that you make a conscious effort to remain non-bias, and accept this story as a story that will determine my hopes of an opportunity to mend the broken hearts of my daughters. They are the ones who ultimately paid the price for the poor choices made by myself and those whom I allowed near them. Please know that my story is purposely written in the state of mind I was in at that point in time, and my intentions are purely to uncover my perspective of what occurred in those fate-changing moments. By doing this, my hopes are that I can be a voice for many people, including four children who had no understanding or method of expressing their pain which was unintentionally, and intentionally, caused by several people, and their lack of knowledge and compassion for humanity.

I have determined that re-living my personal struggles will undoubtedly cause the grief to resurface, but the benefits will surely overpower my pain.

Whoever you are, however you may know me, and whatever your opinion may be, I hope that this story will empower you to find your internal courage to make that one necessary change. The change that your heart whispers to you as you go about your daily routine. The change that will become a transforming gift to our world, which is silently begging to be reborn.

Prologue

Everything is fuzzy. I can't seem to focus. My long brown hair is tickling my face as the wind picks up. It's also interrupting my ability to cast my line out exactly to where I think the fish might bite. Finally, I catch a break from the gusts. After casting my line out and hoping to demonstrate to Zoe and Chloe the importance of eating our catch, or at least making sure it doesn't go to waste, I peer over my shoulder. The white pickup truck is crookedly parked about twenty feet away. It's too quiet, I think to myself. Where are the girls? Where is Derrick?

In a panic, I drop my pole to the ground and quickly race toward the truck. The fishing gear is scattered in the bed of the four-wheel-drive, and the only evidence of my girls is a shoe. A blue and white shoe with the laces untied. It is too small to be Chloe's shoe. It must belong to Zoe. Gazing around, I see nothing. Derrick suddenly appears from the side of the truck and asks me, "What's goin' on?" He yanks his pants up as he steps toward me. His sagging pants are always falling to reveal his boxers. He starts twirling his goatee with squinting, red eyes. He readjusts his baseball hat which reveals his shaved head, to the point of it being shiny. He's the perfect example of a "skin-head".

He wreaks of pot. I can see the heavy smoke swirling out of the passenger side window. "Derrick, where are the girls!?" I ask in a panic. "Honey…" He sighs as if we had been through this. "Chloe is in a foster home, remember?" His statement sounds familiar. I must have forgotten. "Oh. Well, where is Zoe!?" I demand.

"C'mon Elizabeth. Don't get all crazy again. You know where Zoe is." "NO! I don't! Where the fuck is my baby?!" I scream.
His red eyes look to the ground. The silence returns.

As Derrick lifts his head, he gazes to the bed of the truck and nods toward the single shoe laying on its side. As I look over, the wind picks up and the laces begin to sway.

Oh my God. I say to myself. My stomach clenches as I hurry to pick up the tiny sneaker.

"They told me she didn't die, Derrick!" I yell, as a rush of fear overcomes my body. "This can't be true! My little Zoe is only twenty-two months old!" I cry, more to myself. I begin sobbing uncontrollably as my knees hit the ground.

Dear God, Please let this be a nightmare. Please let me wake up! I want my baby back! PLEASE!

I open my eyes to the sunlight seeping through my townhouse window. I am soaked with sweat, still feeling the terror from the nightmare.

With tears streaming down my face, I sigh, simultaneously with relief and grief. I know that today will be one of those tough days. The lingering feeling of pain and sadness from my dream will follow me around for the remainder of the day, and I'll have nothing on my mind except for my babies. I'll also be wondering why my subconscious always seems to bring Derrick into my nightmares as the villain. I sit across the table from him, in deep thought, watching him devour his breakfast.

Never, did I believe that there would be a day where I, Elizabeth Jeter, would live through the events of one of the dramatic novels I loved as a child. I lived through not just one short novel, but a much longer story, with an extra twenty chapters to prolong the agonizing pain. These stories were once my favorite. I read the first one at the age of thirteen.

Chapter 1

My skinny little thirteen-year-old body was pumping with adrenaline. I peered over my shoulder, through my nerdy glasses to make sure that no one else in the class had noticed my shaky reaction. My G-rated literature days were over. I had never read anything so intense. It was like a first date. So nerve-wracking, but incredibly thrilling.

After losing my literature virginity, I started spending all of my free time cozied up in my little twin-sized bed, obsessing over these novels. The characters were all young, beautiful girls in their teens. They all had a disadvantaged upbringing and faced horrible tragedy. Most importantly, they all ended up living in some immaculate mansion with a rich, distant relative that they never knew existed.

My young mind was incredibly influenced by these books. These stories started to create their own lives, building into my subconscious. I was suddenly, completely, infatuated with tragedy as well as thinking up various ways of becoming rich like the girls in the novels. At the age of thirteen, I was going through the obituaries in the local newspaper, hoping to find a rich relative that would leave me their estate. I also put together a flip-book of the future mansion I wanted to own in Palm Springs.

If I wasn't romanticizing about death or tragedy, it was money I was thinking about. Or boys. The thought of boys would take over about a year later. To say I was a little mixed up...well, that would be an understatement.

My first year of high school was a long one. I was quiet and reserved and always thinking that my peers were looking at me and whispering behind my back. I had a boyfriend for most of that year. We were both loners. I would have, most likely, enjoyed my first year of high school more if I hadn't been so caught up in being loyal to him. I had a natural desire to be submissive and completely faithful to any boyfriend I had, starting when I was only twelve. It was almost as if I was living in another century, where women were married off in their early teens, and just had to accept their fate. I must have been born with an old and lost soul, not to mention a stubborn one. The last month of school that year was when my wild streak started. I suddenly broke up with the boring boyfriend and decided that I was going to be much more popular than I had been. I started hanging out with more friends and I was feeling more confident than I ever had.

The snow had finally melted, the sun was just right, and the fresh mountain air brought me to the exciting thought of summer vacation! Something about the sun warming up our cold, icy town had the instant effect of waking me up and getting my blood pumping. The winters were always much longer than the summers. It is almost like becoming free after hibernating in a cold, harsh cave for half the year. For most of the school year, we were restricted to staying indoors and wearing snow boots with double layers of socks. Sometimes, I would put garbage bags over my

2

socks to make sure that the snow didn't soak my feet once I trudged my way into the heated classroom. No more clanking chains on the tires of cars, driving painfully slow down the highway. No more shoveling driveways and suffering through stiff, painfully icy hands, and no more stress over walking to the bus-stop with fear of slipping on black ice in front of a crowd of students. Summer had finally arrived.

The energy at school was elevated, and every student had an eager and excited anticipation for the last bell to ring. Three months of tank tops and beaches could easily put the grumpiest teachers in better moods.

On the last day of school, my rebellious group of friends and I thought it would be a great idea to acquire some forty-ounce beers and have a barbeque. I had a small group of friends and, just like me, they were careless and wild. My fraternal twin sister, Malory, happened to be tagging along, as well. We were really nothing alike. Mal was usually not the type to hang out in a wild crowd. She was quiet and preferred hanging out with her pets, rather than humans. Her room was like a jungle. She had a huge, obnoxious bird that I hated with a passion. Every morning at the ass-crack of dawn, this thing would caw like it was being strangled. I wished I was the one doing the strangling. I am convinced it did this just to torture me. Her snakes gave me nightmares on a regular basis. We had separate rooms for a very good reason.

Mal was not fond of my friends; she thought they were annoying and dramatic. She was usually pretty good at putting that aside for me, and faking a smile when she had to. Today was one of those days. The sunshine must have been bright enough to even get Mal in the mood to socialize.

3

Kate was a girl I had met my first year of high school. She was constantly complaining about some serious life dilemma that she made sound more like a mid-life crisis than an adolescent issue. One week she was pregnant, the next week she miscarried, and the next week she was going through early menopause. Half the time, I didn't even know if she knew what was true or not. She and I had a few particular things in common though; we both loved to drink and flirt with boys. Kate was about my height; five feet four inches. She had the biggest boobs ever and bleached blonde hair. She was curvy, with a butt that could knock down a sumo wrestler. Boys loved that about her.

Megan was the snotty one. She was hilarious, but snotty. She was tall, blonde, and gorgeous. I had become close friends with Megan in seventh grade. She was new to my home economics class and I had decided to take her under my wing. We instantly became almost as close as sisters. She had high standards and loved to give guys a hard time. Megan loved to try new things and was always up for almost any sort of trouble.

As for me, Elizabeth Jeter, I was a small one-hundred fifteen pounds with long medium-brown hair, and I was frequently told that I had perfect lips. I was in love with my flawless figure and I began to notice boys drooling over me as I came out of my shell after getting rid of that boy I was dating. I liked the attention. I wanted to feel special and be liked by the boys around me. For the most part, I was bubbly and friendly, but I also had a somewhat passive-aggressive personality. I was mostly passive until something annoyed me enough to cause a major melt-down. (When I was five, a little girl asked me about twenty times over if I would be her friend. After saying yes for the nineteenth time, I just couldn't handle it anymore. I started viciously whacking her with my plastic softball bat to shut her up. She ran home crying. To this day, I still feel terribly bad about that).

My little group and I were all talking in a circle in front of the gym about who we were going to invite to our shindig. That's when I met Josh, a senior at my high school. He overheard us talking and strutted our way. The tall, handsome senior confidently informed us that he would be joining the party. Coincidently he lived about twenty feet from the back of the high school and that was where the party was to be held. Now, we were all really excited. We walked to the location and soon we were smoking, drinking, and cussing up a storm.

After chugging half a beer, I began to feel that liquid-courage pump through my veins. Whenever I caught a buzz, I also caught a case of extremely enhanced self-confidence. In fact, I believed that I was so ingenious that no matter what idea I came up with, it would always turn out in my favor; that I was an exception to the rule of consequences. Looking around, trying to figure out if Kate or Megan already had dibs on any of these boys, I began to assess which boy might be the most attractive and mature. Josh, the handsome and confident senior, caught my eye. It must have been his tropical, deep, baby blue eyes that were glancing my way every few seconds. It also could have been how I adored the height on this guy, or maybe just his talkative, confident, friendly personality. He was about six-foot-two and, to me that symbolized protection. His confidence made it seem as if he was in total control. All of the boys in my grade were just too short. Some of them still had squeaky voices…and that just annoyed me. My beer-buzzed brain had me fantasizing about the freedom that comes with turning eighteen. I pictured our new, white, picket fenced home, and our little babies playing and laughing. I had this fuzzy beer-induced idea that Josh just might be the one, and fantasized about what it would be like to tell him I was pregnant. I saw him smiling and happy, holding me in his arms. Where the hell did that come from?

I was only fourteen.

When the party died down and the light-weights passed out, Josh walked me home about a half mile down the road. I was excited to know that he lived so close to me. That would make it easier for me to pursue him. He led me up the two wooden steps to my front door. It was an awkward moment. I didn't know if he wanted to kiss me goodnight or just see me off like just another meaningless girl. Before I could think much more about it, Josh wrapped his long arms around my waist and told me that I had the most beautiful eyes he had ever seen. He called me sweetie before kissing me and saying goodbye. This was the first time a man had spoken to me with such sincerity and respect, not to mention that Josh was a clean, yet passionate kisser. I could not stand it when a gorgeous guy was a sloppy kisser. I was excited at the prospect of kissing him again.

I immediately developed feelings for Josh. He treated me as if I were a grown woman; something I had wanted to be for so long. I was sick and tired of other people thinking that they knew what was best for me. I wanted to be ahead of the game. I wanted to have more than any other girl my age, even if it meant finding it in an outrageous way. Josh made me feel like I had a chance to become an adult sooner. I stumbled to my room and fell asleep with a smile.

I woke up the next day to a knock at my door. Josh casually walked in and started chatting away. Ok, good…he still likes me,

6

I thought. I was happy to see him, and I was sure that my mom would like him too. I was right. He fit into our family perfectly. Right away, Josh was great with helping out around the house when he visited; he raked up pine needles in the backyard, and he loved to cook when anyone in the family was hungry. Josh was very talkative and made a great first impression.

Josh was tall and skinny, always dressed in a plain white tee-shirt and jeans. I couldn't believe a handsome and mature guy wanted me. No other boy in our grade had facial hair and a deep voice like he did. I was happy to have successfully found a man. Being with Josh lifted my self-esteem and gave me the confidence I had been lacking. He made me feel like I was worth it. Josh made me feel loved and adored and wanted. I felt as if I was finally whole and needed by another person.

Our first serious conversation came after the first time we had sex, and was introduced by him. It was the age factor. I assumed that because he was a senior he would be about seventeen. He told me he was nineteen. I wondered if he was a little too old for me, but quickly erased the thought from my mind. I was nervous about telling him how young I really was. I decided to do some rounding. I boldly told him that I was fifteen. I was still two months away from that but, in my teenage mind, it was close enough. He sighed with relief and said that he was hoping that I was at least fifteen. I ended up telling the truth a few weeks later. By that time he was already hooked and had said the "L" word, so there was no turning back.

We were together every day, for every possible minute. Our young relationship never felt young, it always felt mature. I thought I was in love with Josh. I knew I was in love with the idea of getting out of my house as soon as possible. I couldn't STAND the thought of facing high school and dealing with my annoying sisters and moody, over-worked mother for three more years. I wanted to play house. I wanted to play house in my own house. I wanted to play house for real.

Officially a couple, coming up on our five-month anniversary, Josh walked me to the chain-linked gate that began the path to my first day of high school as a sophomore. He kissed me and said he would be waiting there for me at the end of the day. As I approached, my friends gave me a look of curiosity and slight confusion. They never thought that I would take a one-night-stand so seriously.

I attended my scheduled classes and could hardly wait for the last bell to ring. Sure enough, Josh was waiting for me at the gate. He had a turkey and cheese sandwich in his hand, knowing how hungry I would be by the end of the day. He always stayed true to his word and had my back. That made me love him even more.

Later that evening, my oldest sister, Lilah, stopped by the house. She had been cleaning her apartment all day and wanted me to help watch my two-year-old niece, Summer. Although she had been scrubbing her floor, she still looked pretty, as usual. Lilah was blessed with a perfect complexion, high defined cheekbones, auburn silky hair, and the perfect lean figure. In her early twenties, she had left home about a year earlier. She and my mother had gotten into some serious battles over some serious, and some not so serious, issues. The house had become much more peaceful with Lilah at a distance, although I occasionally missed her quirky humor. She had met a man the night before while drinking with her friends at the casino, and he wanted to take her out again. She spoke of Huey like he was a true keeper. He was even a doctor! Gross. He must be like thirty something! I thought. Why my twenty-one year old sister was attracted to this old man, (I was later to discover he was in his fifties!) I'll never know.

"I have school tomorrow and I have to do homework. I want to hang out with Josh tonight too." I told her. She looked disappointed, but was understanding. She called the house about an hour later. "Huey says he will pay you to babysit and you can just hang out with Josh at my apartment." she said excitedly. "Of course I'll babysit!" I told her.

What I was really thinking was: I will have all of the alone time in the world with Josh now! We won't have to be sneaky about having sex! This is GREAT! It turned into a weekly job, every weekend. Lilah and Huey spent their nights at clubs and playing poker. Lilah sometimes didn't return until ten in the morning. I would tell Lilah that Josh had left when it got dark and slept at his own house. He would only come by to 'visit' and bring food. This babysitting gig ended up giving me plenty of time to play house.... exactly what I wanted.

Josh and I were becoming very serious, very fast, and on a totally new level.

Chapter 2

Not long into the school year, my health class teacher, Mrs. R., announced that it was time to take home the simulated baby dolls for our 100-point assignment. I had seen other students walking around with these dolls and I always thought that they looked so dumb. I thought this would be more of a hassle than anything. A week later, I was waiting in line at the end of the school day, about to have my doll issued to me for the weekend. It was pretty awkward accepting a fake baby and being expected to hold and treat it as if it were real. When I picked the baby up the first thing that I noticed was that it was actually heavy. The baby probably weighed about eight pounds. The second thing I noticed was that it smelled so good. It smelled like baby powder, clean and fresh. The teachers must have cleaned it and doused it with baby powder to give it a more real effect.

As a child I had periodically adopted a variety of baby animals, so I figured that it couldn't be too difficult to deal with this doll that wasn't even real. One of my first pets was a tiny mouse that I stole from the pet store. I stole Rupert out of fear that he would be fed to a snake. Mal told me that there was no way he

11

would survive because he was just a few days old. I took this as a challenge and spent my last twenty dollars on a small cage and cedar. I set lit candles next to Rupert's small cage every night for the first week to help keep him warm and cozy. Rupert kept me company for the next six months. After coming home from school one snowy day, he was dead on my floor and torn to shreds. The family cat, Astro, (I called him Ass, for obvious reasons) had ripped my little friend to pieces. I ran downstairs, hysterical, to my mother, who asked my pet-expert sister to clean the mess. She did, with no argument. I think she felt bad for me.

Over the weekend, I took care of my "baby" when it cried. I had been instructed to insert a key into its back to calm it down. This baby simulator put ideas into my head that caring for a baby would be as simple as turning a key. I quickly started to enjoy carrying the baby around with me and pretending that I was a mommy. I wanted to practice, and I wanted my doll to be real. After I turned my doll into class the next week I became much more interested in my health class. I wanted to learn more about babies.

It was about six o'clock on a Friday night, and as if we were already living together, Josh and I were making my niece, Summer, a grilled cheese sandwich for dinner. Lilah was, once again, heading to the casino with her doctor boyfriend. I had finally met Huey, grey hair and all. He was oddly friendly, but I still thought he was way too old to be dating my sister. It grossed me out, but I loved Lilah and wanted her to be happy. It was just another babysitting night and Josh was getting bored. He invited his older brother, Jed, to come over with his fiancé and their six-month-old baby. I had expected them to be in their twenties, at least. Jed was twenty-one, and his fiancé was only sixteen. Dawn was a really nice girl and she seemed like a very happy mommy too. Her little baby girl was the cutest thing I had ever laid eyes on.

As I was listening to Dawn talk about the new neighborhood she and Jed were living in, an idea exploded in my mind like a rocket blasting into the night. This was the best idea I had ever come up with! As Dawn was talking I attentively nodded and smiled. I excitedly thought to myself I'll have my own baby! My mom will have no choice but to kick me out! Jed and Dawn made it look so easy. It almost looked fun. My newly acquired vision was that of my new family living together in an adorable little apartment. I saw a happy baby and a husband that worked hard every day to support us. I was a happy housewife wearing a polka dot apron and making cookies with the new offspring. My vision lacked many aspects of reality. I never saw crying, spit-up, dirty diapers, or marriage confrontation. It was a perfect fantasy.

For a long time I had been plotting ways to move out of my mother's house early. I wanted to be an independent adult so desperately. I wanted to get married and have babies and live in an adorable house, with no parent to answer to. This new idea of mine quickly became an obsession that would change the course of my entire life. I started spending my days coming up with ideas to expedite my goal of becoming pregnant. I first searched online.

At the age of fifteen I learned about fertility and the science behind it. I researched different tips and methods for "TTC", or trying to conceive. I was very secretive and subtle about this mission of mine. I printed out a chart to track my periods, so I would know when I was ovulating, and hid it under my bed. I started taking my basal body temperature and drinking an ingredient in cough syrup that was rumored to help. I had a plan if I was caught and questioned about anything: The thermometer and

13

cough syrup were under my bed because I felt like I was "getting sick". No one can argue with that, I thought to myself. I started eating a ton of broccoli. The folic acid in broccoli is supposed to help prevent serious birth defects. I drank extra water and tried to avoid drinking alcohol. I was preparing my body for what I knew it could handle. I was treating this as an adult would. This preparation only motivated me to go to any length to make moving out of my family's house possible.

I became obsessed with finding more stories about getting pregnant. I found reality shows on television that documented couples who were having a baby for the first time. My small fourteen inch television set had a timer and I set it to power on every morning at nine. I had to have all of the information I could possibly get. I researched the subject with true diligence. These couples on the reality shows were much older than I, but that was never considered in my mind.

I watched a movie on one of those Women's Network channels about a fifteen-year-old girl who accidently became pregnant. I watched the movie intensely; nothing in the world could have disrupted my attention. See, I tried to rationalize …it's not all that bad. It happens all the time! There's a movie about it! It's not like I'm only thirteen or something. I had concluded that fifteen was the earliest acceptable age to have a baby. This movie did not scare or intimidate me; it gave me even more ideas and desires to become pregnant. It was a glamorous thing, from what I could tell. I was already mature and grown up enough to make my own decisions. Or so I thought.

After watching show after show and browsing the web for hours on end looking for ways to become pregnant, I went to the shed in my mother's backyard, where Lilah had left Summer's old baby items from when they both lived at home. Lilah had become pregnant when she was a senior in high school. I was only eleven at the time and I was so stunned I could hardly reply to my mother when she announced this. The only words I could mutter in response were, "Lilah had sex!?" I was just about insulted. I look back now and realize that I was probably mostly let down. My big sister was supposed to stay perfect forever. She was very popular and had the funniest sense of humor. She also had a true innocence about her, and I was confused how a person could hide such a big thing. Sex, to an eleven-year-old, is a completely foreign topic that does not have any immediate reality to it. I thought that I would, for sure, wait until I was at least thirty. I honestly didn't even really understand how it worked.

I wanted to see what I could find in the shed to prepare for my desired baby. I hauled an entire crib and a mattress up the stairs, into my messy closet. For days I looked through and sorted bags and bags of baby clothes. My mom and sisters hardly noticed what I was doing. If they did notice and ask I would explain that I was just doing some cleaning because the shed was a mess. I did tell them the crib mattress was in my room so that Josh didn't have to sleep on the hard floor for the nights that he was too tired to go home. Josh occasionally spent the night at our home, once my family grew to love him. The rule was that my bedroom door remained opened and he slept away from my bed, on the floor. We were more excited about the fact that we were trusted enough to do this, rather than actually spending the night together. On weekends Josh was usually either too drunk to walk home, or arguing with his alcoholic mother. We were patient enough to reserve most of our inappropriate contact to times when we knew we would not be caught.

Josh pedaled up on his bike when I was outside folding baby gowns and sorting through items that I didn't want and would be donated. I neatly folded up the baby outfits that I found to be acceptable, put them in my purple duffel bag, and hid it in my closet. Josh looked at the tiny pink dresses and socks. "We should have a baby, that would be so cool!" he said, only half kidding. That gave me butterflies and encouraged my quest to become pregnant.

By the end of summer vacation, Josh was out of high school and working at an oil-change auto service station. I had not told him my plans. There were times that he mentioned how awesome it would be to have a baby, but nothing direct. I took his indirect comments as approval. Josh was never concerned with using condoms or birth control either.

I began to plan our future together as parents. I would occasionally look at the local classifieds to see the rent rates for apartments. I constructed a budget for us, but neglected to take into consideration utility bills, auto insurance, medical insurance… pretty much everything important. I stole pregnancy tests from the local department store every month for four months. They always came back negative. But I am doing everything right! I would say to myself. Giving up on getting pregnant after several negative pregnancy tests, I decided that I would not take another one until my period was at least three days late. I was sick of being disappointed when the tests came back negative.

School was tiring, and I was getting sick of waiting to be free to move out of my house. I became desperate for a break. I wanted to spend even more time learning about becoming pregnant, and school was getting in the way of that. I decided that I could probably at least get a week long break from school if I could find

16

a way to get suspended. The best way to make that happen was to be involved in a physical altercation. I picked a fight with a girl in my grade. She called me a bitch in the hallway after the lunch bell rang. I dropped my books and attacked her. The fight lasted only a few minutes but there were no school employees who witnessed it. I was bummed. I ended up getting Saturday school once word of the fight spread to the teachers. My plan had backfired and I was pissed. The girl I beat up came to school the next day with a considerably bruised face. I couldn't get myself suspended on purpose, even if I tried.

To charge things up and relieve boredom, Josh and I invited a crowd of friends over to Lilah's house on a weekend when we were babysitting, and had them bring some beer. Summer was put to bed and the party started. Josh and I were drunk and acting foolish with everyone else. As I was running up the hallway staircase to relieve my full-of-beer bladder, I suddenly gasped from the terrible pain of menstrual cramps. Shit. I am definitely not pregnant! Again.

Josh went to work early the next morning. I was nauseous and hung over, but I managed to make it to my last class at school, after my older sister gave me a guilt-trip and convinced me to go. Fifteen minutes in, I decided that I was too sick to focus. I walked home and crawled into my fluffy, comfortable bed.

Laying there, I thought about when my last period had been. I pulled the chart from underneath my bed. With a shock, I realized that I was already four days late! I jumped out of bed and hurried into the bathroom. I pulled out a pregnancy test that I had been reserving. It was blue and white, and holding it gave me an adrenaline rush. I read the directions for a tenth time, and tried to avoid peeing on my hand. When I sealed off the pee-soaked tampon looking thing with the cap, I brought the test back into my

17

room. Sitting on the floor, in front of the mirror, I put my make-up on and fixed my hair into a ballerina-style bun. I hated looking like crap when Josh got off work. I always wanted to look nice for him. I waited about ten minutes before I nervously looked back at the test. Picking it up and holding my breath, a pink line stared back at me, telling me I was pregnant.

Chapter 3

Shaking and gasping on the floor of my bedroom, I was scared and confused. I had so many fantasies about life as an adult and doing whatever the hell I wanted any time of the day. But they were just that: fantasies. This was real. There was officially a life growing inside of me. There was no turning back. The reality of the situation suddenly brought upon me a dark cloud of guilt and fear. I began to wonder how my family was going to react. I had a feeling that I wasn't going to be as in control of my life as I wanted. Staring at myself in the mirror, I quickly understood that this was permanent and I could not go back. This was the moment that changed the direction of my heart, mind, soul, and spirit. I was now following a new path that was going to be far more advanced than I ever could have known.

Once I calmed down from the shock of the positive pregnancy test, I casually asked my mother to drop me off at Josh's work, so I could walk home with him when he was off. She said that would be fine. She was extra nice to me on the ride there. Watching the road, not knowing that her fifteen-year-old daughter was holding, in her pocket, a test confirming the existence of her second grandchild, my mother chatted about mundane, everyday things. I started to feel sad and guilty. I knew that she was going to be hurt and let down when I told her. There was nothing worse than seeing my mom upset. I hated to see her cry. It rarely happened, but when it did, it broke my heart. I would soon have to face telling my mother that I was also going to be a mother.

Josh was busy working when we pulled up. Covered in black shiny oil, as usual, he looked over and smiled when he saw me. He asked his boss for a five minute break to walk over to the gas station with me for some cigarettes. My face must have been telling that I was upset and he asked me what was wrong. I cautiously pulled out the positive pregnancy test and held it up for him to see. His expression wasn't happy, but it wasn't upset either. He shrugged as if he almost expected it. He didn't seem like he was too scared or worried either. I think he may have been in shock. I waited at the picnic bench that the guys at the shop used for lunch breaks until it was time for Josh to clock out.

One of his co-workers, Derrick, was making me wish I had waited to tell Josh the news and just stayed at home. Derrick was in his mid-twenties and always hitting on me. I could never tell if he was joking or serious, and it made me uneasy. I had a brief flashback to a few months earlier when Josh convinced my mother to let me go fishing with himself, Derrick, and Derrick's brother, Donnie. My mom asked Josh for all of the details and the exact location. Since Josh did not have a car, Donnie picked Josh and I up on the sunny Friday afternoon. Derrick would follow later in his own car. Donnie had a small pick-up truck that we all had to squeeze into, up front. It was a bit awkward sitting between Josh and an older man whom I barely knew. Donnie had long hair, down to his jaw, and looked like a mix between a hippie and a hobo. He

22

seemed like the stoner type, but was always nice and personable. The thing about Derrick and Donnie, was that they both knew how to make astounding first impressions. They were very engaged in conversations, and always made sure to add in some sort of humor. Donnie was about ten years older than Derrick, although Derrick looked older than Donnie. They were an interesting pair.

After making it to the fishing spot and getting the gear out and set up, Josh and Donnie opened the cooler right away and started drinking beer. Derrick arrived shortly after and was diligently focused on his fishing instead. He brought his obnoxious friend, Jimmy, along. Jimmy had already been drinking when they arrived. I wanted a beer too, but didn't want to ask Donnie because I didn't know him well enough. Josh saw the longing look of thirst on my face and handed me a beer, knowing Donnie would not mind. I was still fourteen at this point. I was excited that these older men were so accepting of my age and didn't mind me drinking with them. It made me feel like I was a part of the "grown-up" club.

While the four men were drunk and I was more than buzzed, we started to pack up because it was getting dark, and Donnie said that if he had any more to drink he would not be able to drive. Goofing off, and having silly, drunk conversations while packing up, we were all gathered around Donnie's truck before parting ways. Jimmy was openly hitting on me in front of Josh. I never took it seriously, knowing that he was in his mid-twenties. He couldn't possibly be serious, I was thinking. The topic of boobs was somehow brought up, and Josh began bragging about how perfect mine were. "She probably doesn't even have tits, she's only fourteen" Donnie proclaimed. Offended that a person was challenging my womanhood, I replied "Oh please. You would be

23

surprised." Not knowing that I had placed myself into a vulnerable situation, Jimmy excitedly challenged me. "Yeah, right. If they're so awesome then prove it!"

Standing in the dark, surrounded by four men who were all much older than me, I looked up at Josh to defend me. "Show 'em." He confidently said. After debating and arguing about exposing myself to old, horny men for what felt like hours, they were not about to let up.

I purposely postponed the challenge as long as I could, because it was getting dark, and the darker it got, the less they would be able to see. My liquid courage was not serving me so well this time. It was finally almost completely dark, and my buzz was wearing off and making me tired. I just wanted to go home. After the hundredth beg and plea, I finally lifted my shirt as if I were a confident showgirl from Vegas, performing her routine. "Yep...those are brand new." Donnie casually said as he was exhaling his cigarette smoke. "Damn! Junior has it made!" Jimmy practically yelled. (Junior was the nickname given to Josh by his coworkers because he was the runt of the group) Derrick looked annoyed and almost mad. "Macy is making lasagna tonight, I'm outta here." he said as he got into his car and drove off. With the flash show over, I was pleased to be accepted into this "grown-up" crowd, but my stomach ached and I knew that God was very sad with my decision. My youth and innocence were further tainted by this choice. I blocked it out of my mind and pretended that it was just a bad dream.

Millions of thoughts raced through my mind while I sat on the wooden bench at the tire shop. There were even more conflicting emotions. I did not know if I should be happy or if I should be devastated. The more I thought about my child, the more I grew

24

attached to it with each passing minute. I knew who this person was, and I knew that this person was necessary to the world. This person was going to be beautiful, perfect, and needed. I was not the only one that would need this person. Their purpose was much more powerful than that.

As a mostly mature adult, I have learned that what is meant to exist will exist. It will find a way to embrace this world if God decides that it needs to be here. Through this process, I felt God was with me. I heard God's whisper of encouragement to move forward, to not allow any force to stand in my way. I felt safe and cared for, even when I was at my loneliest moments.

When the next morning arrived, I knew deep down that I was going to keep this baby. No person or force would have the power to change my mind. I had a vision of what my baby was going to look like. She would be beautiful, tall, and skinny, with stunning blue eyes and a big, bright smile. And, of course, she would have long, dark hair. Yes, that would be her. I knew who she was long before I met her. I knew who she was from the beginning of her existence. I held off telling my mother the news for as long as possible. I just didn't want to face it. I was worried that she would be mad.

Only a few days after finding out that I was pregnant, I was exhausted by the time the last bell rang at school. I would be enrolled in Driver's Education class after school for the next few months and having to sit and watch documentaries on the consequences of drunk driving was no picnic. That was when the seriousness of my age was brought to light. I began to feel uneasy thinking about the fact that I was pregnant and I wasn't even old enough to get a driver's license! I was no longer feeling confident about anything, or secure with what I thought I wanted. That day I drove myself home, with Mr. Morris in the passenger seat, stomping on his brake pedal every time I went too fast or didn't look over my shoulder. I was already feeling sick, and the bumpy ride was not helping. I walked into the house and slouched onto the couch. I was happy the day was finally over.

Idly watching a talk show discussing cheating husbands and their lies, I barely glanced up when my mom came through the front door. She quickly looked at me and spoke. I was surprised by what came out of her mouth: "Are you pregnant?" Well, shit. That was a pretty straight forward question, I thought. I used my usually topic-avoidance-technique: I rolled my eyes. "No. What the hell? Where did you hear that?" I said, trying to sound offended. She then explained to me how she had received a phone call early in the day from one of my teachers who had overheard other kids talking about it. I was confused as to where that came from. I hadn't told anyone except for Josh! My mom sighed with relief and walked back to her bedroom to do her usual nighttime ritual of watching the news in her pajamas and eating ice cream. I knew I could no longer hide the truth from her. I had to face what was happening.

The next morning I woke up feeling sick and nauseated. I came to the conclusion that I wasn't going to school…my life was over anyway. I would spend the day at home trying to figure out how to tell my mom the truth. Josh came by the house on his lunch break to see how I was feeling. We mutually decided to spill the beans to my mom. Both of us were much too scared to tell her in person. We decided to write her a letter. Later that night, after spending an hour carefully finding the right words to scribble down, Josh was brave and took the letter down to my mother's bedroom. He came back up to me, and we waited in fear for her reaction. My room was directly above hers, so we could hear most of what was happening below.

"Gosh, damn it!" She was so mad that she didn't come up to talk to us for what felt like a lifetime!

Finally, she came up to notify us that we better figure out what the hell we were going to do and how we were going to take care of this. I had no idea what she meant by "take care of this". Neither did Josh.

The next morning I decided not to go to school, again. I slept until about ten, and when I woke up, I still didn't get out of bed for a while. I started to think about my options, how sad it would be to choose abortion. I knew that nothing could ever make me do such a horrible thing, but the thought of it still made me cry. I heard my mom coming up the stairs and I buried my face in my blanket. She walked in and sat on my bed. The second she started to lovingly twirl my bed-head frizzy hair, the flood gates opened. It was as if the Hoover Dam had collapsed. Something about sympathy from a parent makes it much more difficult NOT to cry. She explained to me that I still had to go to school. She asked me what I wanted to do about the pregnancy. I told her that I would rather choose adoption over abortion. I told her that I did not want to feel guilty for the rest of my life for killing an innocent being.

"Well, if you and Josh are that serious, maybe we can look into you two getting married then." That statement brought me peace and comfort. I just needed her support in this. I knew that without her help I would be lost.

The events of the next few days changed the feeling of the situation. I finished up my Driver's Ed, but refused to attend my other classes. I did not want to deal with people talking about me every time I walked into a room. My mom scheduled an appointment with my school counselor to discuss my options. The counselors told me that I could keep attending my regular classes, go on independent study and do work from home, or attend the Young Parents Program. I wanted to stay at home. I had this idea that it would be safer to hide away from the world. What I did not know was that the world, and the people in it, could not be avoided.

Later that day, a detective from the police department came to my door, looking for Josh. One of my high school counselors had called the police.

Chapter 4

A loud knock on the door startled me as I lay on the couch. I had just gotten home, tossed my backpack on the floor and fell on the couch. I was tired and definitely not in the mood to deal with those annoying churchgoers wanting to invite themselves in to talk about ways of avoiding going to hell. According to a Mormon family I was acquainted with, I was already there. About two months pregnant, I felt bloated and just wanted to unbutton my jeans permanently. I walked through the atrium to the front door to see a tall, dark silhouette standing behind the blurry glass. I had no idea who was there or what they wanted. I slowly and cautiously opened the creaky door to be greeted by a man wearing a badge that read Police Department. "Great. What did Josh do to get himself into trouble last night?" I thought to myself. Josh had been out drinking with a few friends the night before to "celebrate" our future baby.

The police officer looked to be in his late thirties with dark hair and a kind smile. He announced that he was there to speak with a Ms. Anna. "That's my mother and she is in school right now" I replied. He asked me what my name was. Upon introducing myself, he took a small notepad out and located his pen to scribble down notes. I was confused and starting to become worried. A rush of fear made me weak when I heard the words "How old is your boyfriend, Miss Grace?" I stuttered as I attempted to think of a way out of telling the truth.

I am a horrible liar when I'm nervous. For that reason, I just spit it out. "He is nineteen, sir" I said. I realized that the only way to fix this potentially terrible situation was to become extra sweet and appear to be mature. I wanted the police officer to see me as a nineteen-year-old; I did not want this man to see the situation for what it really was and have Josh arrested. Josh was only four and a half years older than me. I really did not think that it was that bad. People would just have to be understanding. After all, he is stepping up to the plate and supporting me, right? Why would anyone believe it to be necessary to take away the father of an innocent child and maybe soon to be husband?

The officer replied with a series of questions: "So, how did you meet Josh? Is he supporting you through everything? How does your mother feel about this? Did you ever feel pressured into sleeping with Josh, Miss Grace?" I answered every question simply and in a way that I thought would only be beneficial enough to keep Josh out of jail.

The officer was very nice about the entire matter, and as he retreated down the driveway he said that as long as my mother did not wish to pursue criminal charges, the case would be dropped. Later in the day, I overheard my mom on the phone with the officer. She was speaking as if she was upset and confused, but she did not mention anything about agreeing to have Josh thrown in jail. I did not expect that she would; she loved Josh like a son and she knew that his intentions had always been right. I was happy

32

that the dilemma was over. I did not even fathom the fact that this particular dilemma was only the first out of hundreds to follow.

I discovered that I was pregnant in the beginning of September, 2002. It took about two weeks to get the guts to tell my mother, and then it took another two weeks to officially tell her my decision to carry the child. I played it off as if it was just another simple issue, and life was to carry on as usual. I did not want to talk about the subject because I already knew what my decision would be. I knew my decision would stir up some anger in my friends and family members. My innocence was entirely gone to them. What was done was done. There was no way in hell that I was going to agree to have an abortion. Most every person I knew was attempting to convince me that if I kept this baby my life would be over. These people had no clue that I wanted this baby; they had no clue that I became pregnant on purpose. I was being harassed about having an abortion almost every day. I was almost to the point of frustration that I just wanted to agree to shut everyone up.

A bright Saturday morning blazed through my bedroom window and made a failed attempt to ruin my slumber. Thank God for my thick purple curtains. As I was painfully trying to open my eyes I was startled when I heard a knock on my bedroom door. "Who is it?" I groaned. "Hi Elizabeth, it's Huey." My older sister's boyfriend called from the hall. "Can I talk to you for a minute?" I was pretty irritated that, out of all people, Huey was at my door. Jeez, does he want to put a move on me too? Maybe Lilah's last birthday really did him in and it was time for a newer model. Dirty pervert. Why the hell is he at my door! I was thinking. I told him that he could come in, and I was relieved to see that Lilah was following behind him. At least with Lilah there, it wouldn't be totally creepy and awkward with him in my bedroom.

The second he started talking I knew what his intentions were. He talked about a former Colleague of his who used to perform abortions. "It's quick and painless. Most Doctors will use metal instruments, but Dr. Smith only uses leaves from a seaweed plant. He soaks the leaves in a saline solution before the procedure, and he uses it to scrape out the contents of your uterus. It won't cause cramping or pain because the seaweed is so soft."

I wanted to vomit as he was holding up his fist, as if his wrinkly hand, with grey knuckle hairs, were my uterus. He was trying to show me how a seaweed abortion worked, and I was lucky enough to get a reenactment to go along with it. Seriously, what the hell was that all about anyway? Seaweed…abortion…? Seriously dude, you're an idiot. I affirmed. I gave him my attention, but never confirmed to him what my decision would be. I thought it was incredibly insensitive of him to refer to my unborn child as "contents". I could not understand why terminating a pregnancy was so freely accepted as an option, almost to the point of being favored.

This was my child we were talking about. I consciously chose to give this child life. It should be no person's decision as to who lives or dies, especially as a pure and perfect creation of God. Our world needs more innocence, more purity. This baby would forever be a part of me, who I was, and what I stood for. I knew this child's soul. I truly could envision the face of this child. I saw the smile, heard the laugh…and felt the embrace. These feelings were so intense that they could not be classified as only feelings. It was more than that. It was more than a natural inclination to

34

protecting the human species. It was more than a teenage girl with baby fever. It was destiny. It was meant to be. She was meant to be. Unable to see past the next year, I did not quite understand how important this small angel would eventually become to the world, and some of the desperate people in it.

I was getting sick and tired of people being so adamant about this abortion thing. They were acting like it was just another common thing to do and that it was perfectly okay. I chose to become pregnant! Making that decision then following it up with an abortion would be completely senseless, and it would ruin me forever. I had to find a way to get people off my back. I knew exactly what I needed to buy` some time.

"Thank you for calling the Women's Clinic, this is Chelsea, how can I help you?" the receptionist said. "Yes, I need to make an appointment to have an abortion done." I confidently announced. The receptionist asked me a series of detailed questions, and I noticed that her voice sounded very caring, but somber. That must be a really horrible job; making appointments to schedule the killing of innocent babies, I thought. After answering all her questions, she confirmed that it would be four-hundred dollars. "That will be fine" I stated, knowing that I would not need to worry about coming up with the money. After she collected all of my information, it was time to schedule the appointment date. I told her that my schedule was open, so she could just choose the day. "Will October 6th be okay, Elizabeth?" she asked. "Sure! Go ahead and book me." I said. Chelsea must have thought that I was a whack job with how enthusiastic I sounded about this abortion. I just wanted to hurry up and get off the phone so I could announce the fictitious death of my baby, and have a moment of peace.

This particular scheduled day was not just any day. This was my mother's birthday; a day that I would recognize for the rest of my life.

I took this as a clear sign. This was not a coincidence. This was God trying to show my mother that this baby was meant to live. When I informed my mother that I scheduled my appointment to have an abortion, she seemed relieved. She did not seem to care much about the fact that it was on her birthday. She even said that she would give me a ride to Reno, where it had been scheduled to be performed. After talking with me about my options and having some time to realize that I was truly pregnant, I think she just wanted this problem to go away. She was going through the stages of grief; shock, denial, bargaining, and anger. I was eagerly awaiting the acceptance stage. I knew that I would have to be very patient.

What my mother did not know was that I had only scheduled this appointment to get everyone off my back. There would be nothing left for anyone to say if they thought that I had accepted the decision to terminate the pregnancy. What could they say? "Congratulations" or "I'm sorry" I was outsmarting them. I was way ahead of the game, and for a moment I felt a small twinge of control again.

Over the next few weeks I was at least able to live in peace without any harassment. The few days before my appointment were when I felt the tension arising once again. The day before, my mother confirmed that she was giving me a ride to the clinic in Reno the next morning. I just couldn't beat around the bush any longer. "I am not having an abortion, and no one is going to change my mind. I will never be able to live with the fact that I took an innocent life, and I would rather choose adoption if it comes down

36

to it. I would be reminded of the fact that I KILLED my baby every year, for every birthday you have!" I boldly told her this from the door of my bedroom.

The screaming match began. She had prepared herself to get rid of the dilemma and forget about it, she did not expect that this "dilemma" would be permanent, and not go away so easily. "When my baby is older I will tell it that you wanted me to kill it!" I angrily yelled at her. "Good! You're an idiot!" She screamed back. "You have no idea what you are getting yourself into!" The yelling back and forth lasted about ten minutes before was over. Neither of us heard much of what the other was saying. My ears were ringing. Not too long down the road, my mother apologized sincerely for things that were said. I ended up apologizing back. I have learned that it is never wise to make any statements based on emotion. You only end up hurting the people you care about.

I was sad, but I was also relieved to know that my decision was strong, firm, grounded, and exposed. I was sad because I knew that my family was disappointed in me for the decision I had made. At least life could carry on without questions up in the air. I did not even bother calling to cancel my appointment. I thought that the clinic deserved to lose money from my no-show. I thought it was an evil place that killed innocent beings on a daily basis. For all I cared, the entire building could burn.

Chapter 5

Finally having made the clear decision that I was going to have the baby, it was time to decide how I would finish school. I received a phone call one Friday afternoon from a woman with a very friendly and cheery voice. I had no idea why this woman asked for me. "Hello, is this Elizabeth!?" She asked. "Yes, this is Elizabeth. Who is this?" I replied with an almost snotty and annoyed tone. I was so down in the dumps that others who seemed extra happy just pissed me off. I wanted to be happy too. I wanted to be excited and brag about my future baby. The excitement went out the window entirely when I realized that because of my age I would not have support from my community for this pregnancy. It was shameful in their eyes. I desperately needed an adult to as least act like they cared.

"Hi Elizabeth, this is Mrs. Snow! I am calling to find out if I can work with you to help you finish your high school education. I understand that you want to do independent study for your pregnancy, but we have a really great program here. It is called the

Teen Parents Program, or TPP. You will come in for half of the day, we'll feed you breakfast and lunch, and we have a great daycare along with parenting classes for the remainder of the day to help you get ahead. Can I meet you in person?" she pleaded. Mrs. Snow genuinely sounded thrilled about this program.

It also seemed as if she may have had several teen parents turn the program down, based on the hopeful, yet uncertain, tone that I sensed. I did not know much about the program, but I knew that it was in the building down the street from the football field, and away from the main campus. I always thought that the kids who went there were the troubled drug addicts. "Um…sure, I guess I am willing to come take a look at the place" I unenthusiastically said. I told her that I could come in on the following Monday to give it a test run. I had no clue what I was getting myself into, but deep down I really needed the extra support, and I was hoping that I could find it there.

Once the shock of my decision started to fade my mother slowly got back to normal with our relationship, and the old conversations that we usually shared seemed to level out. When this happened, it was like a breath of fresh air. It had made me sad and stressed to have negative vibes and unspoken anger consuming our home, and it honestly had put my life and happiness on hold for a bit.

When I explained, to my mother, the conversation I had with Mrs. Snow she seemed happy about the whole idea and agreed that it would be best to give the Teen Parents Program a try. I needed all of the advice and education that I could get, as far as becoming a teen parent was concerned. When I was in my fantasy world, trying to become pregnant, my vision of actually being pregnant was way off from what reality proved to be. I did not see myself as a teen mom. I saw myself as an adult with her first baby on the way in a society that had no objections to it. I was wrong. I was delusional and confused. I understood that I would face criticism and the disapproving turning of heads, probably on a daily basis. I came to the realization that if this was going to work in my favor in any way at all, I was going to have to become the best teen mom that I could possibly be. I was going to need to rise above and beat the statistics. The first step that needed to be taken was to graduate high school.

The morning of my first day at the new school had arrived, and I was tired. I remember feeling so overwhelmed from just moving one muscle, not even an inch, to get out of bed.

Since I was a baby, I have always hated mornings. Any small disturbance quickly sets me off like a Mentos dropping into a Pepsi; fast, intense, and sizzling over the edge for a good while. I recall getting ready for kindergarten on a distant October morning.

That was a frustrating morning. I was only five, and all I knew was that I had to hurry up and put my socks and shoes on. We didn't want to be late for the bus. In a hurry, I found my sneakers tangled up on the brown carpet in my bedroom, grabbed a pair of socks and carried my stuff to the bathroom where I plopped down on the floor. I had recently learned to tie my own shoes, so I wanted to make sure I had no interruptions as I was focusing on this delicate process. I never actually made it to the shoe part. THOSE SOCKS! They were plain white socks; I thought I would have no grief with them. The second that my tiny little piggy's attempted to snuggle into the end of these particular socks, my heart sank. "THESE ARE THE WRONG ONES!" I was hysterically trying to explain to my mother that the seams at the end of my toes felt funny. She was dumbfounded. For the life of her, she could not

41

comprehend why an almost microscopic seam would bring me to such hysterics. I later learned that I sat on that bathroom floor for an hour twisting the socks around my foot, over and over again because I could not get it right. One way or another, those obnoxious seams would, very rudely, bombard the cracks of my toes. My mother, at that point, was at a loss. We missed the bus, we were late for school, and I was at the maximum melt-down point that any five-year-old could possibly be.

Finally, as if the good lord sent down a guardian angel to guide her, she pulled both socks off of my feet, yanked them inside-out, quickly put them back on my feet, and all was well. The day was free to resume as usual.

As my mother was driving me down the street from our home, which was less than a mile from my new school and the TPP program, I became nervous and I had no idea what I should expect. She was dropping me off for the day, and I was hoping that I wouldn't have to be stuck in a room with a crowd full of annoying and immature screw-ups. I walked into the portable classroom building and was surprised that it pretty much looked like a regular classroom. I was greeted by Mrs. Snow, who was warm, friendly, and enthusiastic. She had short, grey hair but her skin appeared youthful, and her personality even more so. I liked her right away. She asked me a few questions and had me fill out some forms, but I never felt any sort of judgment coming from Mrs. Snow. Her heart was no doubt in the right place.

There were only three other girls in the class. They were all Hispanic, and speaking to each other in Spanish when I walked in. I was worried that they might be talking about me. One looked to be about six months pregnant, and the other two did not appear to be pregnant at all. I assumed their babies were at the daycare Mrs.

42

Snow had told me about. After I was introduced to the class, I found out that the girls were all older than me. Great. I really am an idiot for getting pregnant. I could have at least waited a freaking year! I was thinking to myself. The girls were sixteen, seventeen, and eighteen. I didn't think that I was going to fit in very well. I didn't see how I was supposed to make any friends if they never bothered to speak English to me. I felt left out.

After finishing the paperwork and getting acquainted with my new surroundings, I sat down at one of the tiny chair-desks that were lined up in a row, facing the whiteboard. I wondered how in the world I was supposed to wedge my pregnant body in one of these things once I got big. It was inevitable. I just hoped that my boobs would stay preserved.

A few minutes after taking my seat, one of the cafeteria kids, wearing a dorky looking hair net, entered the classroom, pushing a cart full of trays. Oh, joy. It must be breakfast time. My downer-self was thinking. Mrs. Snow handed each of us a tray and a carton of milk. Breakfast included a cinnamon roll and an apple. I devoured the cinnamon roll. It was amazing. It made me thirsty, plus, I was always thirsty in the mornings anyway. I opened the carton of milk, which I normally didn't consume as a beverage alone and chugged away. I drank the entire carton in about ten seconds. This is when I realize that, along with being pregnant, I would be forced to suffer through the crappy symptoms. I felt like the milk was about to come back up.

My fear of throwing up came back to me full force. As I was feeling an adrenaline rush and hot flashes racing through my still tiny body, I decided that I could not throw up in front of the class on my first day. I would never be able to live that down. I would be known as the girl who puked. I would be renamed something like pukie, barfie, upchuck, yacker, pottie-hugger, or who knows! I tightly closed my eyes and mouth, slightly dropped my head, and focused on my breathing. I meditated my way out of throwing up. Thank God! That was definitely a close one. I was only ten weeks along, and this was clearly only the beginning of the hellish symptoms.

After Mrs. Snow issued my books to me and gave me my first homework assignments, it was almost lunch time. "For lunch we head down to where the daycare is and spend the rest of the day in groups doing projects or sharing our concerns as teen mothers" she announced. This had me thinking: Great, now I get to spend the next few hours listening to pathetic pity stories. We all walked to the daycare center as a group. It was away from the main classroom and down a gravel road. The building was hiding behind trees at the end of the football field, and to get there we had to walk down an extremely steep hill. I thought it was pretty ridiculous that they had pregnant girls make this walk. Maybe they secretly wanted us to slip and fall. Obviously, this daycare was hidden away from the rest of the school. Of course the school and the town wanted to hide this shame. South Lake Tahoe is a tourist town; a town that caters to outsiders by offering them brightly lit casinos, boat rentals, shopping, and concerts. The façade, put on for the tourists annoyed the shit out of me. Beauty can be deceiving.

Finally arriving at the daycare, we walked through the front door. The building looked old and beat up. There was what appeared to be finger paint on the windows next to the door. I wasn't sure if the art work had been done by the kids being cared for, or if the kids-with-the-kids had done it. Either way, it made me feel like I was in first grade again…except I was pregnant. I hoped I wouldn't be asked to contribute to it. It was just strange.

44

Lunch was served but I really did not want to risk the possibility of throwing up, so I just picked at my tray. There were a few babies in the room and a few more young mothers as well. Some of the mothers chose to study at home and just take their parenting classes at the school. When Vanessa walked in, I was relieved. At eighteen she was six months pregnant, and she spoke English and appeared normal. She was cute and seemed to be much more mature than the other girls. I immediately made conversation with her and asked her questions about morning sickness. Meeting Vanessa definitely perked up a day that had been long and confusing.

After everyone finished lunch and the mothers tamed their screaming babies, a public health nurse walked in. She was going to lead the day's group activity and ramble about the importance of breastfeeding. I couldn't tell if the chubby nurse was naturally nasally or had a cold, but her loud breathing got on my nerves and I wanted to chuck a box of tissues at her head. I did end up learning some valuable facts on breastfeeding though, and I had already decided that I would probably nurse my baby for at least a year anyway. That is what Lilah did with her daughter, so I figured it was the right thing to do. She actually nursed her daughter until she was almost two and, at that time, my snotty pre-teen-self gave her hell for it. I thought it was so gross to let your kid, who could walk and talk, help themselves to dinner on your boob. I was completely merciless to her. Sorry about that, Lilah.

Before it was time to go home the nurse, Valerie, pulled me aside and asked me some really detailed questions about my pregnancy. I was polite and answered to the best of my ability, but became irritated when she made the most unnecessary statement I had ever heard. "Well, you're still under twelve weeks gestation, so you could still have a miscarriage. Oh, but don't worry- it's just a little clump of cells right now." I wondered if she was thinking that I would have a miscarriage. Why else would that statement ever have any sort of use? I disliked the pig-faced nurse from that point forward.

The day was just about officially over, and I was finally free to walk home. The walk was not very long, but I was incredibly lazy and easily became irritated if my mother or sister couldn't give me a ride home on some days.

Walking through the front door of my home I was sweaty and out of breath, but I was actually excited to tell my mom about my day. She was in the kitchen making something that smelled amazing and I began to blab away. Even though I was super tired from my long introduction to my school life as a teen parent, I still felt that I should attend the Teen Parents Program on a regular basis. It would be the only place that I could turn to, where my situation was completely accepted; the instructors had such a positive outlook.

It would be a while before my mom started to fully support me, and my sisters were just as confused with the whole thing as I was. Although my mother was clearly still in shock over the situation, and trying to find a way to process what was going on, she did her best to put on a smile for me and encourage me to stay in school. That made me happy.

Chapter 6

Over the next few weeks Josh continued to work at the oil change place, making minimum wage, and I got myself into a routine with my new school. Because I was now pregnant, as I had once so desired to be, Josh and I naturally wanted to spend even more time together. I wasn't babysitting Summer as much, Lilah must have been getting worn out from all of her casino outings. Babysitting had really been the only time that Josh and I had privacy and the chance to spend our nights together.

Considering the circumstances, a couple of unusually uneventful months went by. I was about four months along. I could still easily hide my condition if I wanted to, but I didn't need to bother. It was a small town, and everyone talked. I knew that hiding the situation would only prolong my anxiety about people's reactions to it anyway. Having to tell friends why I suddenly left school was bad enough; I dreaded telling my extended family. Most of them lived a couple hundred miles away, and it was going to have to be a phone call that broke the news. I knew it would be hard because I loved and respected them so much.

My Grandparents spoke with my mother frequently, so I knew that she must have told them already. Any time I would hear her talking on the phone, I would intentionally hide. I either went to the back yard where it was easy to hide behind a gigantic pine tree that must have been hundreds of years old, or I would run out the front door and go on an aimless walk down the street. I hated confrontation. On one occasion, I heard my mom coming towards the stairs with her clanking heels tapping against the hard wood floor. I heard her reply "Hang on, let me see if I can find her". It was time to move fast. I rolled off my bed in a hurry, almost landing on my face, and somehow performed a stunt-man style leap into my huge closet. I hated my closet. I always had evil spiders creeping in the dark corners. This was a situation where I had to suck it up and hide, like my life depended on it. I was just not ready to talk to my Grandparents, for the fear that they would be disappointed in me. I loved them both so much and was so sad thinking about how I must have let them down. Walking through the door to see an empty bedroom, my mother investigated no further and walked out. I am never going to be able to handle this all, I thought.

Finally, about a week later, I gave up on my fight to hide and I forced myself to be available to talk when my mother was on the phone with my grandparents, during their usual Tuesday night chat. Handing me the phone, my mother could see the worry on my face. "Hello?" I nervously said.

Immediately following my shaky greeting, their all-too familiar voices were like music to my ears, and helped put me at ease. "Hi honey! How is our girl!?" My Grandparents always sounded enthusiastic when I spoke with them. They always made me feel so loved. I was thinking that our conversation was off to a good start by the way they were maintaining their normal conversational style. I carried on and spoke as if I wasn't thinking about the pregnancy, as if nothing had changed. I desperately wanted to keep our relationship as stable and happy as possible. I wanted to keep our relationship, on my end, as innocent as it had always been.

There was only one statement that my Grandpa made that brought an immediate lump to my throat: "Honey I am really disappointed. Really disappointed." I had to fight like a warrior to hold back my tears. I never wanted to disappoint my Grandma and Grandpa. That was just about the only negative sentence I had ever received from either of them and, to this day, this still remains true.

My Grandparents always uninhibitedly gave Mal and I the kind of treatment that only royal princesses should receive. This started the day we were born. Not only did they spoil us with presents and chocolate pudding; they offered us their constant attention, every minute that we were together. They were much younger than most grandparents that I knew of; only in their fifties. Our Grandpa was technically our Step-Grandpa. He never had any biological children with our Grandmother and, I suspect, that could partially explain their love and attention to Mal and I. My Grandpa even named me while I was still in the hospital. When I was little, I would obsessively brag about this. They truly cared as deeply for us as any parent would care for their own child. Out of every member of my extended family, my grandparents have always had the tightest grip on my heart-strings.

I had let them down, and it broke my heart. Getting off the phone, and saying our goodbyes, I set the handset on the kitchen table and ran upstairs. I didn't want my mom to see me crying. I was crying out of guilt for being such a disappointment to two people who always took such good care of me and loved me so very much.

I waited until Thanksgiving to tell my Dad. I wanted to wait as long as I possibly could. I knew it wasn't going to be a pleasant conversation. I really did not want to hear his criticism. Even my mother avoided telling him. We avoided him for about two months, so I was sure that he suspected something strange was going on. When he called on Turkey Day morning, my mom answered the phone. It was, at first, a normal 'Happy Thanksgiving' conversation. It turned bad the second she told him. "What the HELL Ron! Maybe if you ever showed a fucking interest in her life she wouldn't be in this situation!" I heard my mom scream. The two of them were like fire and ice. They just did not mix. I have no idea how they were ever together long enough to create me. For the record, I really try to avoid thinking about that.

Our parents split when Mal and I were just babies. When we were little our dad would come pick us up on the weekends. We were only about three years old, and he had a small apartment across town. I remember that I would always get excited when I saw him pull up. I loved it when he picked me up and gave me attention. He was tall, and I thought it was so cool to be so high up in the air in his arms. My twin was the opposite. She was never very thrilled about leaving our mother for the weekend. The story we were told is that he threw a sandal at her forehead and she, being pissed, locked him out of the house.

Our mother is not a person who you would want to piss off. She can definitely hold her own and is not afraid to show it. Apparently, our dad came back to the house a few hours later begging for his can of soup he had left. To this day, Lilah still talks

52

about how bad she felt for him that night. I am guessing that he did not really return for just a can of soup. He probably wanted to resume his normal family life and seek forgiveness for that sandal shot. Needless to say, their relationship was over.

Lilah has a different father. She didn't get to meet her father until she was seven. Gabe was with my mother since she was only thirteen. He joined a church that was extremely set in their ways and strong with their beliefs. For some reason, Gabe disappeared and decided to marry another woman from the church. I don't know why any man would ever do that to a woman as beautiful and loveable as my mother has always been.

As I grew older and met my older sister's father and his family, I realized that everyone involved really seemed to have good intentions, and things just turned out the way they did because they were probably supposed to be that way. Every person has lived through a unique experience and through a totally different reality. I try not to draw conclusions about other people or situations unless I am actively involved.

I don't allow myself to judge based on what happened in the past. I am no longer okay being that way. I never could have guessed that I would end up being in some of the most horrifying situations that life can possibly offer.

After Gabe left, my mom was on her own at nineteen-years-old, with a little baby and not enough help. At that time, she was living in a mid-sized California city that was pretty ghetto. She was only there because of our Great-Grandmother, who we called Grams. Grams was one of the only family members able to help her out at that time. After sitting in a dirty town for a few months, she just couldn't handle it any longer. She hopped on a bus to

Tahoe with her last twenty dollars. The one-way ticket took her four hours away.

My mother went straight to the Casino to see if she could find a job. She was hired on the spot. It was going to work out for her, after all. My mother took a huge leap into the unknown to offer her baby girl, Lilah, a better life. In turn, she offered all of her daughters a better life.

Even after living in Tahoe for twenty-one years, I could easily still sit and stare at the lake and admire the beauty that the deep blue sparkling water would imprint permanently into my soul. That sparkling imprint would soon transform into a deep, black, suffocating scar that would follow me for the next six years.

On the phone with my dad, the criticism started. "What the hell have you been doing, young lady?" my dad questioned in a deep, matter-of-fact tone. I was silent for a few seconds. I had pre-determined that if my father was not going to offer me any comfort, love, or support, I was simply going to hang up on him.

"Elizabeth, are you there!?" he growled. "Yes, I am here. It is what it is, dad… I can't go back, so I am going to work on finishing school early" I attempted to confidently say. "The only thing I can say that you're doing right is not getting an abortion. God doesn't approve of that" he reminded. I explained to him that an abortion would never be an option for me. "So, what the hell do you think is going to happen? How are you going to support this kid? Do you really think that this Josh guy is going to give you what you need? You have really screwed up big time." I was done with his negative scolding. It was Thanksgiving, and he was ruining it. "You know what!?" I finally screamed. "I am not going to put up with your shit! If you can't be supportive then I'm just not going to speak to you anymore!" Tears began to roll down my face. I pushed the red button on the phone and it was over. I attempted to hold back my tears as my mom and sisters came into the hallway to see why I had been yelling. They all comforted me and gave me hugs to try to calm me down.

I didn't know if I was crying because my dad was an asshole, or if I was crying because I was an asshole for hanging up on him. Regardless of the reason, my heart was aching. This particular incident did prove one positive thing, however; it showed me that my mother and sisters really did care. They were there to support me for the long haul. Once I dried my tears, I stuffed my face with my mother's amazing Thanksgiving dinner. For the moment, all was well. Except that Josh was nowhere to be found.

Chapter 7

My mother, sisters, and I were lifelessly lounging on the couch, satisfied from stuffing ourselves with turkey to no end, when I heard the squeaky front door of the house open. Joy. Josh must have decided to join the family, I thought. Sure enough, he stumbled in with that, all too familiar, glossy look of disorientation on his face.

He was drunk…again. I was definitely upset. I could not figure out why, of all days, he decided to get trashed. He had been at his mother's house, or his second-house I should say. He went back and forth from my home to his mother's in a lost transitional limbo for quite a while. I knew that any time he was with his mother for a prolonged period of time, he was drinking.

Hilda was an alcoholic. Although a functional drunk, there was no hiding her addiction. Her name was Hilda. It fit her perfectly well. She was loud and obnoxious and overwhelming to be around, even when she was not drinking. Her alcoholism, however, can be somewhat justified. When Josh and I first got together we were spending time together at his mother's house when she and her new fiancé were on a short vacation.

I noticed that on the floor was sitting a small brown chest with a few children's items neatly displayed on the top. Josh noticed me looking at the chest and took this as an opportunity to share with me a very sad piece of family history.

His name was Beau. It was a bright, sunny Friday and the boys were all excited and getting ready for their first trip to Disney World. Beau was about three years younger than Josh, and Jed was about two years older than Josh. Hilda had three boys, all with the same man, and it sounded as if the family was intact and happy. After a normal six-year-old tantrum, Beau was instructed to spend time in his bedroom to calm down. After getting everything together for the trip, Josh went to get Beau. Opening the bedroom door, he realized that Beau was gone. In a panic, nine-year-old Josh searched the room high and low, only to notice that Beau's fishing pole was missing and the window was wide open. Without thinking twice, Josh leaped out the window and ran down the path that led to the boy's favorite fishing spot.

When Josh arrived, he discovered his little brother face down in the river. The rocks, water, and hills had been too much for a six-year-old to safely maneuver through. Josh screamed, and found someone who called 911. The rescuers were able to transport Beau to the hospital, still breathing, but otherwise lifeless. After spending days on life support, Beau was gone. His brain had endured too much irreversible damage.

I was saddened to hear this story. I wondered how Josh still remained such a happy and kind person. I was shown pictures of the sad experience, and one particular picture broke my heart. It was a last goodbye picture of the big brothers by Beau's bedside, broken, and in tears. The wooden chest was all the family had left of their youngest member. It was filled with toys, stuffed animals,

58

and cards from Beau's classmates. I vividly recall Josh sharing this experience with me. Maybe it was the universe preparing me for the tragedies to come, or maybe it was a sign for me to hold on, fully and completely, to everything special to me.

Although Hilda angered and annoyed me, it was now clear what had shaped her into the person she had become. What bothered me most, though, was that she had most likely been a negative example for Josh from the time that Beau had passed away. In Josh's world, getting wasted on a nightly basis was normal. It was what his mother did, naturally, he sought her approval.

Rising from the couch where I had been laying with my mother and sisters, I moved toward Josh, standing just inside the open front door. Josh looked at me like a deer-in-the-headlights, and I instantly knew what he had been up to. Naturally, I wanted to take care of him and just fix the situation. After closing the front door, I grabbed his hand and attempting to drag him up the stairs and away from my family. He was so incredibly inebriated he was grabbing onto anything and everything along the way, to keep his balance. At the base of the staircase he grabbed my mother's wooden hutch, knocking every glass valuable off with a shatter. I heard my mother yell something as I continued to lead him up the stairs. We managed to make it to the top with incident. Before he could make his way into my bedroom, he fell flat on his face in the hallway, and broke his nose. Gushing blood, and having broken expensive items along the way, he lay in the hallway as my mother raced to see what was going on upstairs. This is where everything took a plunge.

"What the hell is going on, Josh!?" My mother yelled. "Shut up you dumb bitch." he slurred "Yer just jealous you can't have me." My jaw dropped and I almost burst out laughing. That was very out of character for Josh to say. My mom was so mad that her lips tightened and the look that I usually ran from came over her face. "That's it. I'm calling the cops." She stated. She followed through and called the police. On one hand I couldn't blame her, but on the other hand, I was extremely scared and unsure if this was the right thing to do. I tucked my drunk boyfriend into bed. He made a horrible attempt at taking off his pants to sleep in his boxers. His boxers came off with the pants. I hurriedly tried to get his pants back on so the poor cops wouldn't have to deal with a naked drunk, but I failed. He was nothing but dead weight. This is where my sympathy for Josh ended. He was about to embarrass not only himself, but me too! I gave up and walked out of the room and accepted our fate.

The police sobered Josh up enough to get him in cuffs and escort him down the stairs and into the patrol vehicle. Josh went to jail for vandalism.

That night, I felt very lonely and let down. I felt betrayed by Josh and as if my mother just didn't understand. I didn't know why Josh felt it was necessary to ruin Thanksgiving, and I didn't know why it was necessary for him to be arrested when I depended on him so much. The only thing I could do for comfort was to write in my Journal.

Dear Josh,

I have never felt so empty and sad. Right now I am laying in my cold, lonely bed and you are laying on concrete in a jail cell. I don't know why things had to turn out so bad tonight. It was supposed to be Thanksgiving. Why would you ruin a holiday, out of all days? I am at a loss and don't know what to do. The drinking has to stop. I can't allow this to continue. We have a baby on the way, and that is no environment for a child to ever be in. I don't want to break up, but I think you need to stay at your mom's for a while. I know that you are probably just as nervous as I am about having a baby, but that is no excuse to binge-drink every day! You are not the same person when you drink. You break my heart every time you stumble in drunk. Either way, I still love you and I always will. I can't imagine having to do this without you, but I am going to have no choice if you can't get sober. Please, just do it for me? And if not me, then get sober for your baby?

Love always,

Your future wife

I did not intend on giving Josh this letter. I just had to release my pain. I was unsure of what the future would bring. I was unsure if he could truly handle the responsibility that would soon be bestowed on him. Finally, around 3am, I fell asleep. I fell asleep, sad that Josh was probably sleeping on a cold concrete floor. I fell asleep, sad that our semi-stable circumstances had just been slammed down with a dark and cruel bottle of whiskey.

Chapter 8

The seasons were changing as fast as my pregnant belly. The storm from Thanksgiving died down and life returned to a somewhat stable routine. Josh learned a lesson - for a while anyway. He still drank, but not as much as he had been drinking with his mother.

Christmas morning arrived, and deep down I knew that it would be my last Christmas as a child. This would probably be my last Christmas living with my mother and sister. This would be the last time that I would be woken up at 4am by my twin sister to sneak down the stairs to retrieve the beautiful stockings that our mother had always carefully and thoughtfully put together. Every year, she would spend so much time and thought finding us gifts that were perfect for who we were, individually. The gifts, from books to chocolate and diaries were always wrapped and tied with an artistic touch that only a perfectionist could master. They were beautiful. The most beautiful part was the love and energy that she had put into them.

After excitedly, but also somewhat sadly, going through my gifts on my unmade bed, I stuffed four truffles into my mouth and lay down to go back to asleep. Mal woke me up a few hours later as Lilah and Summer arrived. As a family, we opened our gifts, cracked jokes, and unknowingly enjoyed our last Christmas together that would resemble a normal family and childhood. We didn't know it at the time, and would not have wanted to.

A short time later, Josh came over. I had a stack of gifts for him. I had really gone all-out. After learning the story of Beau's death, I had a deep sympathy for Josh and I wanted to make up for his loss and sad childhood memories. I wanted to make up what his mother could not. This was a big factor in how I treated our relationship from that point forward. I just wanted to love and help him. I wanted to show him what a safe and happy family was like. I wanted him to someday see how poorly of a lifestyle his mother was leading, and how horrible it could be for him to follow her. Everyone can hope. I hoped until there was none left.

After Christmas break I resumed school as usual. I had finally made friends with the Hispanic girls that I thought hated me. They were really nice, and usually pretty damn funny. They made it easy to laugh at the small things that would normally bother me. I had a great sense of belonging and I knew that no matter what obstacles were in my way, the Teen Parents Program offered plenty of resources. They even had a counselor come once a week to talk with us individually for a half hour. Her name was Rosa. She was in her early thirties and I loved her personality. She reminded me of a hippie as well as a responsible and concerned mother. I could talk to her about anything that was bothering me without worry of judgment. I usually was able to do the same with my mother, but it was nice to have a person that was not in my immediate life. Between the support from school, my immediate family, and Josh, I was doing exceptionally well. I was going on seven months. My body had changed, but I wasn't too concerned. I knew that was the sacrifice of my choice.

One day, out of the blue, my mother announced to me that she wanted to throw me a baby shower. I was initially unsure about the idea. I was wondering to myself, who in their right mind, is going to want to attend a baby shower for a fifteen-year-old!? I was embarrassed. It was okay for me to be openly excited about my baby while I was at school or when I was with Josh, because everyone else was in a similar situation. I was worried about what friends of the family and even my friends would think.

The following week, during Josh's lunch break, he took me to my final ultra-sound appointment. We were both excited, and betting on a boy. There were so many girls in my family already and I wanted to be the one that broke the dramatic cycle of nail polish and pre-menstrual moods swings. However, deep down, I did not think that we were having a boy. I just played along to keep Josh's spirits up. As we were walking down the long hallway to sign in at the hospital, Josh was talking about what he would teach his son. I only had one thing on my mind: I had to pee, bad. My doctor had instructed me to drink as much water as I possibly could, before the appointment. He said this would cause my bladder to push my uterus up into a favorable position for the tech to take measurements. I was gagging through episodes of severe acid reflux, and I was sure that I would pee everywhere. At least I could blame it on my water breaking. I was somewhat relieved to have a backup excuse.

The male technician squeezed ice cold gel on my pumpkin shaped abdomen. He firmly pressed the probe directly on my bladder. I grimaced in pain, but decided to tough it out. After fifteen minutes of torture, the part we had both been anticipating

67

arrived. "You kids want to know the sex of your baby?" he casually asked in a monotone voice. It was as if he had been trained to ask the same questions, and was bored with it. "Yes, please." I said in the calmest tone I could. I was extremely eager and excited, but I didn't want to annoy him with my teenage giddiness. He already seemed annoyed.

After scanning for about two minutes, we were given the news, sort of. "I am not one-hundred percent positive, because the legs are crossed… but if I had to bet on it, I would say it's a girl." Josh and I looked at each other and smiled. I was worried that he would feel let down if his dream of having a son was shot down, but the look on his face told me that he was already completely in love with this little girl. I was excited to confirm the vision I had earlier in the year of a beautiful baby girl. I had known it from the very beginning.

Pulling into my driveway, I noticed a few strange cars. I had no idea who would be at our home. It wasn't until I walked in and noticed a stack of bibles on our table that I knew what was going on. My mother had recently started attending a church, down the street. She went to bible study on a regular basis, and she had confided in the pastor about my situation. That night the bible study was being held at our home.

I was introduced to the pastor, along with a handful of other middle-aged locals. They were all very nice. I really liked the pastor. Pastor Gene. He was an older man, maybe in his late sixties. He had a slight resemblance to Santa Clause. His personality fit the character well. Something about this pastor made me feel safe. I felt like I was speaking to a very positive and clean force, almost one of an angel. "I was speaking with your mother, and I wanted to ask you if I could host the baby shower at my home. There is
68

plenty of room and I would really love to help you get things set up." he said. I was surprised that a person who must be so morally and spiritually intact would want to help me, of all people. "That would be awesome! I was worried about how many people would show up and I just wasn't sure how to go about it all." I said, trying to contain my relief. It would be easier to accept a baby shower if it was held by a third party. It wouldn't make me look so stupid and desperate if another person was hosting it for me.

Two weeks before the baby shower I was eight and a half months along. My mom handed me a stack of invitations to send out. I had not thought about who I would invite, and was afraid that it would turn into proof that nobody cared when they chose not to show up. After battling with my self-esteem taking a plunge, and my hormonal brain being extremely emotionally indecisive, I said to myself, Screw it. I sent out an invitation to every person I could think of. I made some phone calls to get missing mailing addresses, then sealed and stacked the envelopes. I was expecting the worse, but truly hoping for the best.

The next week I had trouble focusing at school and I became somewhat overwhelmed. Between being extremely pregnant, and having to show the reality of this fact by attending my baby shower, I was not getting much sleep. I would stay awake until two in the morning reading the novels I had once obsessed over, hoping to distract my busy mind from my fears and worries. After sleeping for only four hours, I would wake up again at six in the morning to waddle down the stairs to the kitchen. I found a particular cereal to be extremely pleasurable. I would drench it with honey and waddle back up to my bed. My insomnia was normal for third trimester fatties to deal with. It was nature's way of preparing for the soon-to-come sleepless nights of caring for a new- born.

Chapter 9

"What the hell, Mal?!" I angrily screamed. I was so mad that I felt tears streaming down my cheeks. The warm, and clearly fresh, dog shit must have been waiting specifically for me. It was in the perfect place, at just the right time.

"What's wrong, Elizabeth?" My mother asked with a concerned tone. "Mal needs to clean her dog's shit off the floor! I just stepped in it and it's stuck between my toes!!" I hysterically announced. This time, waddling with a limp, I rushed to the bathroom and awkwardly lifted my leg to get my foul smelling foot in the sink. The warm water gave the dog crap an enhanced, steamy smell, like it was being boiled for dinner or something. I gagged and, almost throwing up, quickly squeezed the entire contents of the bottle of hand soap onto my violated foot. Standing with my foot in the sink for about fifteen minutes, I hoped that all of the microscopic, disgusting particles of bacteria were gone. I forfeited my quest for cereal and waddled back up the staircase and into my bed (which I hoped wouldn't become contaminated with any hiding feces I surely missed).

The day of my baby shower had arrived. It was a bright and sunny day. Spring was teasing me with the melting snow that always had a beautiful sparkle. My mother and I headed to the pastor's home early. We needed to set up, and make certain appetizers that my mother was determined to serve. It was the first time I had been to the pastor's home. I imagined that it would resemble the typical old person's home; with that brown Tahoe-style carpet, shag length, with orange and green appliances from the 1970's. This home proved my imagination wrong. It was big, beautiful, modern, and very clean. It was located in a part of town where the well-off usually chose to reside. Actually, it wasn't too far from Dr. Huey's house. I learned that the home was provided to the pastor and his family by the church, for the duration of his work.

I nervously paced around, trying to come up with some sort of helpful task, but I was probably just in the way. Pastor Gene must have noticed my anxiety. As the time for guests to arrive neared, my stomach was in knots and I felt seriously ill. Pastor Gene approached me and asked if everything was alright. I casually explained my nervousness, and he handed me a plate with cheese and crackers. He told me that eating would help my nausea and things were going to be just fine. As I was choking down the dry crackers, my first guests arrived.

"Hi guys!" I excitedly said. I was more than happy when I saw that Mal had brought along some friends we had made during our first year of high school. They were all boys, but I thought that it was so sweet of them to show up, considering that most men have egos in the way of allowing them to attend a baby shower. I was instantly relieved that anyone had shown up at all. As the next fifteen minutes passed, more people were ringing the doorbell than

I could keep up with. There was a pile of gifts on the dining table, and the big living room was filled to nearly maximum with guests. There was an even mix of teenagers and adults. They were all friends who had never done me wrong, and the hope that I would still be loved and respected was considerably restored. Josh and I served the beautiful Bambi cake that my mother had ordered. It was so pretty I did not want to cut into it. I made sure to keep the decorations from the top of the cake. I wanted to save them for my baby so she would know how special they were and how excited everyone was about her arrival. I was impressed with the crowd, and the gifts, but I was even more impressed with the effort that was put into this event.

Just like our Christmas stockings, my mother had carefully and lovingly taken her time to make it the best party she could. The appetizers were all miniature. From shrimp cocktail to mini pudding cups, it was all delicious. The games were hilarious too. Watching blindfolded teenage boys scoop cotton balls into a bowl was the best. Even now, as an adult, I am truly impressed that these boys were selfless enough to show their support. So, wherever in the world you may be at this point, I want to thank you for making a difference in my life.

Ending the day's festivities was no easy task. There were so many gifts that Josh and I had to plan how we would stuff them into his old, beat-up Subaru. We finally managed, and once we got home and unpacked, we felt as if we just might be ready to meet our new baby. All that was left to do, at that point, was wait. The more my stomach grew, the more anxious I had become to just get it all over with and not be pregnant any longer. I wanted my body back, and I wanted to meet this human that had been taking it over.

Driving down the slushy highway, my mother asked "What time is this appointment?" "Two forty-five" I tiredly said. I was thirty-six weeks pregnant. I was more mentally ready to have the baby than I ever thought I would be. Physically, I ached, but I knew deep down that my body was resilient and would handle it just fine. Walking into the Doctor's office for a routine, weekly visit, the nurse called me back as usual. And, as usual, she did not say my last name right. How hard can it be? I complained to myself. Most of the doctors and nurses I had seen were very nice to me. I never felt like I was being judged or looked down on. I figured it was because they either became used to seeing young, pregnant girls, or they didn't want their personal opinions to jeopardize their careers. Regardless, it definitely helped to make the process a smooth one.

As the nurse was taking my blood pressure a slight look of concern came over her face. She released the cuff and took it again. She immediately left the room, and walked back in with the attending Doctor. "Elizabeth, your blood pressure is a little bit higher than we would like it to be. I am going to have to order some tests and have you follow up at the clinic across the street. We need to watch you closely, and if this problem gets any worse the only way we can treat you is to deliver your baby." The Doctor was nice, and he did not seem panicked, just a little bit concerned. I did not feel bad, so I was unsure of what was going on. I was actually a bit excited over this information. This meant that, just maybe, I could have my baby sooner rather than later. I had another four weeks of the pregnancy left, but I truly was not thrilled to wait that long.

My mother and I walked over to the lab to get the tests done. Then we met my mom's friend, Elma, at a small Chinese buffet.

74

Elma was always super nice to me, and I always secretly thought that I was her favorite out of my sisters and I. "Lizzy is going to be a mommy! I'm so excited for you, honey!" she said. I could tell that she really meant it. This was the first time that a person spoke my name and the word "mommy" in the same sentence. It gave me a strange feeling. My subconscious knew that I was too young to be a mother. My heart would not let my subconscious bombard the happy moments that were to come. I responded with a shy, yet friendly "Thank you. I am too." Shortly after my response, I felt a bad case of heartburn coming on. I casually pushed my plate to the side and sipped on my hot tea.

We said goodbye to Elma and drove up the street to settle in for the night. I was hoping that my next appointment would bring some sort of news. Any news telling me that I was almost done with the pregnancy would be music to my ears. I became even more anxious and excited later in the night after Josh had come home after work. I began to feel what I thought were Braxton Hicks contractions, but they were coming every twenty minutes. Josh and I sat attentively on the couch for about two hours, hoping that something might happen. Sadly, they faded away by midnight. It was nothing but a big tease. As Josh fell asleep on the floor, I began to fall into a deep trance of thought, as I usually did late in the night. I was wondering what would happen to my baby if I were to die in labor. I knew that Josh probably couldn't handle it alone, and it would be a disaster for his mother to attempt to pitch in. She already screwed up her own children. I had an urgent feeling that I needed to write a letter in the case of my death. At least my wishes would be documented. I quietly pulled my journal out of the night stand drawer I kept it in, and started to write.

Dear Josh,

I want you to know that I will always love you so very much, and I am always going to be with you. I know that you are hurting, but I need you to be strong for our baby. You are going to be the center of her world, and we both need you to be a good example for her. I know that this is not how we wanted it to end, but God is taking care of me, and I am safe and happy. I want you to focus on what makes you happy, and on what makes our baby happy. Please tell her every day that I love her and I am with her. Please remind her that I would not change anything to save my life. If you become tired or overwhelmed, please give our daughter to my mother. Your mom is in no state to take on that sort of responsibility, and our little girl deserves the best - you know this. I infinitely love you and our baby, and I will see you when God calls your name.

Your wife forever,

Elizabeth

Chapter 10

I hated the clinic that my doctor had forced me to make an appointment with. It was a community clinic, and it was smelly and overcrowded. My options to see a specialist were slim, as I was forced to enroll in state insurance to cover the expenses of the pregnancy. When the state had asked for my mother's personal information (because I had resided with her) she just about burst a gasket. She was irritated and insulted that the same office that disbursed welfare payments wanted information from her. She eventually got over it and gave them her social security number to get me on the coverage. Growing up, we did not have a regular insurance plan; any time we were sick or needed any sort of medical care our mom would always make sure that we were promptly seen. She had a way of being classy and resourceful all at the same time. I look back and admire her for this.

The nurse called me back, and I was greeted by two male doctors. I felt uncomfortable and was glad that I had my mom come into the office with me. One doctor was an intern, and the other was clearly a veteran. When he introduced himself, I realized that he was the father of a boy I went to school with. How freaking embarrassing! I thought as he was checking to see if I had dilated. It was mild torture. "You are about three centimeters, and with your permission I would like to strip the bag of waters to help your labor progress. We can't really allow a woman with preeclampsia to remain pregnant for very long." he said. "Sure. Do whatever needs to be done." I replied. This procedure wasn't supposed to hurt but because I, myself, was not finished growing, it hurt like a bitch. Luckily, it only lasted about thirty seconds. I was happy to get dressed and out of the clinic. I didn't feel any different, and I assumed that whatever he had done was probably not going to make anything happen yet. I had never even heard of that procedure, and thought it was probably just an old wives' tale.

Waddling my way back into our home, I started to feel sick and tired. Mrs. Snow had left a message on the answering machine wanting me to go into school to take an important state test that all of the students would have to take. I had scheduled to do my work at home for the last month of my pregnancy, but I thought that I would just suck it up and go in the next morning to prove my dedication to graduating high school. I had it in my mind that I would graduate early so I could start college. I did not know what would become of my future when I began to live away from home. My mother had not mentioned anything to me about moving out, but I knew that eventually we would have to get our own place. Josh, going back and forth, was frustrating to me and it would be difficult to feel like a responsible parent if I was still living with my parent.

I walked into the portable classroom the next morning, at nine. I was surprised when I realized that the classroom was completely full. It was not just pregnant women or mothers. There were regular students in the class taking the exam as well. One of these students was a boy I had hooked up with the previous year. He was a popular kid, and I felt like a complete idiot when he gave me a second glance. I was sure he was thinking Go figure...she's knocked up. I tried to ignore my insecurity and focus on the exam. The first hour I was doing just fine. When I began the next part of the exam my nausea overcame me to the point of searching for a trash can. I, again, meditated my way out of humiliation and quickly guessed on the rest of my answers. I left early, and Mrs. Snow didn't put up an argument.

My mom picked me up in the hidden parking lot by the football field, and I explained to her that I was feeling pretty crappy "You're probably in labor, Elizabeth!" This was the first time that I knew for a fact that she would love this baby. She was as anxious to meet this kid as I was. "I am not having contractions though. It's probably just a bug or something." I stoically replied. As confident as I was, I was forced to re-think my statement when I sensed how confident she was. After all, she did have three children. Two in one shot. She should know. When we returned home I spent the rest of my day on the couch. I was unable to eat because I was still sick to my stomach and it was definitely not letting up. Josh came home from work and I forced him to rub my feet. When nine o'clock hit, we were both too tired to finish our movie and headed up the stairs. He grabbed his portable twin sized mattress out of my closet and kissed me goodnight. Looking back, it was pretty silly that we both had our own twin beds, and his was on the floor. It was like a really screwed up slumber party or something. Curled up in the fetal position, as best as my stomach would allow, I fell into a deep sleep. I was dreaming about giving birth to baby kittens. It was so realistic, but I knew that there was no way I was a cat.

Chapter 11

Opening my eyes, I had to squint to see the clock across the bedroom. It was already three in the morning. I was confused from the dream I was having, and I wondered why I had woken up when I had been sleeping so well. I felt a little bit sick. It was coming in waves, and it was more of a sharp pain than nausea. I realized that these pains must be contractions. They started to come every fifteen minutes, and the intensity was a little harsher each time. I quietly wrote the times down on a piece of paper. I didn't want to wake anyone up until I knew for sure what was going on. I thought it was strange that these contractions didn't hurt; they were just uncomfortable. I was extremely calm, and I laid in bed thinking about how bad it could possibly be to give birth. A strange calm came over me.

Finally, when six o'clock rolled around, I needed to get out of bed and do something to relieve my discomfort. What was worrying me the most was that the contractions had come down to only five minutes apart. I didn't want to put up a fuss and panic though. I didn't want to startle or worry my mom or Josh, mainly because I wanted to take a shower before I went to the hospital. I thought it was very important for me to be clean and primped. This was a special occasion and I was not about to show up in pajamas. I knew that family would be invading the hospital room and snapping tons of pictures, and I did not want my baby to one day see these pictures and how horrible I looked.

"Josh? Can you go ask my mom if it's okay for me to take a bath, and also tell her I am having contractions every five minutes?" I quietly, yet firmly, requested. I didn't want to be mean, but in order to get Josh to fully wake up I had to display a serious side. He was a deep sleeper. "Yeah, sweetie, I'll be right back" he said as he bounced up from the floor, out of my bedroom, and down the stairs.

Only thirty seconds went by before he came back up. "She said as long as your water didn't break you can take a bath." Thank God. I just needed to change my position and do something to distract myself. It pain still wasn't too bad, but I felt the increasing intensity with each contraction. I submerged myself in the bath and it was heaven for about five minutes. The contractions were coming much more closely together. The relaxing bath may have triggered this. I quickly stood up and dried off. I sat in front of the mirror and quickly put my make-up on. I really wanted to dry and style my hair but I knew that I could not spend that kind of time at the moment. I twisted my wet hair up into a bun on the top of my head and changed into a comfortable sweat outfit.

Josh followed behind me as I walked down the stairs. My mom met us at the bottom. "Elizabeth, do you want to ride with me to the hospital so I can hurry up and get you checked in while Josh packs up the overnight bags for the stay?" she asked. "Yes. I was going to ask if we could do that anyway. But we should go because they are kind of close now." I tried to say casually, but my
86

strained voice gave me away. On the drive to the hospital the contractions were more intense and it was miserable sitting in the upright position that the passenger seat forced me to be in. I really had to focus on my breathing at that point. These contractions were just too strong. If I hadn't focused on my breathing, I could have panicked.

At last, we pulled into the hospital parking lot. I hurriedly (almost sprinted) into the entrance. I had to go to the admissions office first, but once I sat in the waiting room I just couldn't handle waiting around. The older lady holding my stack of records kindly instructed me to go ahead and get over to labor and delivery while my mother finished up for me. She must have recognized the look of agony on my face that appeared every few minutes. I was thankful that I was free to go.

"You're six centimeters dilated, and fifty percent effaced." the nurse excitedly announced. I was expecting to be maybe two or three centimeters at the most. I have heard numerous stories from women about how long and tedious their first labors were. Lying on my side in the hospital bed, I looked at the clock and it was eight-thirty. I didn't understand where all the time had gone. It felt like I had been in my bathtub five minutes earlier. Maybe the inability to keep track of time is nature's way of helping women deal with pain. Pain alone is already difficult; having to endure pain with a sense of time to accompany could be a recipe for disaster. I was quite the pro at meditation by this time. I had plenty of practice from all the times I avoided throwing up. I transformed into a deep trance toward the end of my labor. I closed my eyes, and as each contraction peaked, I envisioned myself standing barefoot on the beach as the waves rose, peaked, and crashed down. The waves eased my anxiety immensely. My

87

subconscious did not know what to expect with the foreign, yet natural, forces of labor, but I very well knew what to expect with the waves of the ocean. There was a break, every time. Like my contractions; a rhythmic movement, but never continuous.

Flashing back to the beach and some of my favorite memories; running barefoot and free as my grandparents tried to keep up. My Grandpa sitting me on the counter in the motor home as the first rays of sun glistened from the crashing ocean, helping me drink a small cup of orange juice by myself. I must have only been three years old. Falling asleep to the peaceful waves, reacting to the forces of our planet, is an experience I'll never forget. That sound carried me along my journey of bringing a new life into the world. It was nature working with itself. Even at fifteen years old, I wasn't afraid. I felt like it was okay, and that it was supposed to be happening.

Josh and my mother were the only family in the room. I had a group of friends, along with my twin, sitting in the waiting room. Lilah was still at work, but she had called my mother to say she was heading our way. The clock on the wall said ten-fifteen as the doctor walked in to assess my progress. Rolling onto my back for the exam was horrible. As I was contracting, it was nearly impossible to meditate my way to relief. After all, the doctor was intrusively breaking my water. "Holy shit! That is so gross!" I whined, in shock. There had to have been over a gallon of liquid that came crashing onto my legs and bed! Doctor Howard was trying not to laugh. He was about my mother's age and was very well known in the small town. He carried himself calmly and confidently, which was exactly what I needed to see. I needed a certain, unspoken reassurance and it was as if he could read my mind. "Rub my feet!" I screamed to Josh. I needed something,

88

anything, to distract me from the pain. "I think I feel the head." I said, with panic in my voice.

"You're ready to have this baby." the nurse said.

Chapter 12

Completely unaware of what to expect, I welcomed the idea of finally bringing my baby into the world. Pain was no longer the dominating thought. Getting to meet my baby for the first time was far more important. For the entire pregnancy, I planned to be tough and deliver my baby "naturally"; without an epidural, that is. My mother had twins naturally, so of course I could handle the pain of just one baby. At fifteen, I had no way of even slightly predicting the pain of a vaginal birth. Of course, I knew somewhere deep down that it must not be pleasant. I also did not know the extent of this unpleasantness.

As Josh was holding my right leg, my mom supporting my head, and a young nursing assistant was holding my left leg. I was more concerned with down south (uh-hum) being groomed enough to avoid my peer to the left becoming grossed out. Sure, I was thinking about the pain, but this girl looked familiar enough to the point that I wondered if she had recently graduated from my high school. I was thinking about how embarrassing it would be if she came to the realization that she knew me outside of the hospital room. I hope I remembered to shave, I was thinking as I was having a thirty second break from the nearly continuous contractions. My fear of embarrassment quickly vanished as the next contraction forced a pressure on me that I had never known to be possible. As much as I wanted to stay calm and push this baby out, while still maintaining my dignity, the pain forced a moan from my mouth that was even foreign to me. This moan was not voluntary, it was nature taking its course, by whatever means necessary to keep my body and mind from going into total shock from the pain. The moaning was a minor release of the overbearing pressure. I remember thinking that if I were to grip my mother's fingers tight enough and hard enough; maybe I could transfer the painful energy over to her instead. Focusing on my forceful squeeze was also a slight release to my pain.

Besides my discomfort and the awkward, and completely foreign, sounds that emerged from me, the room was peacefully silent, as silent as it could safely be with medical personnel communicating, anyway.

The doctor's voice broke my inner silence. "Now this is what we call the ring of fire, Elizabeth. It's going to be very uncomfortable, but it is the shortest part, okay?" "Sure." I responded through clenched teeth. Like I had a choice anyway! The only fix to this pain, feeling more like a soccer ball making its way out of my ass, was to deliver this baby. After Dr. Howard explained that he was going to be performing an episiotomy, and first had to numb my perineum with a local anesthesia, I rolled my eyes and slammed my head back onto the hospital bed. What the hell is a perineum anyway? It sounds like one of those gross words. Like 'Volvo', a car I will never drive because of its resemblance to 'vulva'." I almost laughed to myself. The medical terminology was getting annoying. Out of an unexpected nowhere, a great relief

92

came over me. The pressure was still there, but it was lifted up from the deep, torturous hell I had previously been feeling. "Umm…did you just cut me with those scissors?" I shamelessly asked. I was truly curious. It seemed like a mutilation of such extremes would be horribly painful, but it actually was quite the opposite. I'll put it plain and simple: it felt good. Okay…I said it.

Lilah made her way into the hospital room just as I was about to deliver. She looked scared as she ran to the other side of the room, being forced to cross paths with my gaping vagina. I couldn't handle any more of this drama, with my legs up in the air and everything completely exposed. I hated feeling vulnerable. This was definitely the most vulnerable I had ever felt in my entire fifteen years of existence. With another contraction coming full force, I took a deep breath in and pushed with all the strength of my existence. This was the last push before I felt my baby finally exit my body.

I felt as if I would float off of the hospital bed at any moment. It was the most enormous feeling of relief I had ever experienced. This baby, that we had all been waiting so long to meet, was finally here. As the nurse wiped the blood and white greasy stuff off of her little body, I was finally able to look at my baby's tiny face.

"Oh my God, I'm going to cry!" Lilah exclaimed, choking back the start of a sob. My mom was at the baby vital station with my new baby, snapping as many pictures as she could with her newly purchased disposable camera.

The nurse set her on my now un-pregnant belly, and for a few moments I was in shock. I could only rub her head and make sure that she did not fall off the bed while I was attempting to absorb what was really going on. I noticed that she smelled funny, and I wondered if anyone else in the room noticed this as well. Her little cry finally emerged from her hard-at-work lungs as they were trying, with all their might, to offer her the first few breaths of her life. In a daze, my memory still remains blank, except for noticing that she had my lips, a head of beautiful, soft hair, and the sweetest cry I had ever heard.

Before I knew what was happening, my hospital room was flooded with visitors including Josh's family, my high school friends, and my twin sister, Mal. I was even shocked when Josh's mom and her fiancé both gave me a hug and kiss on the forehead. It made me happy to know that so many people actually cared enough and wanted to be a part of this precious, yet controversial, experience. A short time later my mother and Lilah returning with a lunch of fresh strawberries and lasagna from a bakery that I so dearly loved.

After the visitors left Josh went to announce the news to his buddies and coworkers who lived down the street. I finally had time to be alone with my baby, in silence. As she was peacefully sleeping in her bassinet next to my bed, I reached over to gently rub her head. Tears began rolling down my face. I allowed myself to sob with joy.

Chapter 13

Just looking at my new baby girl brought tears to my eyes that were completely uncontrollable. I was so grateful to have this little angel, who looked exactly like me. She made little creaky-door noises, and was so perfect. I had no idea that I could possibly love something so deeply. I had no idea that something so small could fill my heart with so much happiness. She was beautiful and perfect, and I had no doubt in my mind that she had come from heaven. God had sent her to me, and my faith was given strength and certainty because of this. She was mine.

I picked up my little girl and brought her close to my chest. Chloe Lynn would be her name. Weighing seven pounds, at nineteen inches long, she was perfect in every way. It was so hard to imagine who she would become as she grew older. For now, I didn't care. I wanted everything to stay just as it was right then, in that very moment, forever. I had never felt such a rush of euphoria in my life. I held onto my baby girl until I was ready to fall asleep. I gently put Chloe back into her bassinette. I realized that it was nearing eleven o'clock at night and I wondered why Josh hadn't returned to get to know his new little girl yet. As the clock continued to tick I was becoming angry and sad. I fell asleep with a bittersweet feeling in my heart. The bitterness was caused by the father of my new baby, who was nowhere to be found.

About an hour after dozing off, I was rudely awakened by the sound of Josh stumbling through my hospital room door. A strange woman followed behind him. I felt rage come over me. My face must have been turning a deeper red with every passing second. Confused, disoriented, and flat-out pissed off, I could not understand, for the life of me, why Josh had decided to get wasted tonight! And why he thought it would be okay to allow some strange woman to follow him back to the hospital room. Trying with all my might to contain my mounting rage, words spilled out of me, "What is going on? Where have you been? I have been waiting here by myself for hours." The way Josh looked at me as I was speaking clearly told me that, once again, he was totally trashed.

The woman behind Josh suddenly stepped into the room, and started speaking even faster than I had moments earlier, "I'm sorry I didn't introduce myself right away, my name is Devalin. I'm friends with Josh's mom, isn't she great by the way? Anyway, I gave Josh a ride back here because I didn't think he should drive. Oh yeah, I also wanted to ask, do you want me to sneak you a margarita? I mean, it must have been some hard work you just went through, huh? There's nothing like a cold refreshing drink to take that pain away!" This hideous woman began hysterically cackling. No wonder she was friends with Hilda, I thought. Birds of a feather…

Her obnoxious laugh woke Chloe up. I practically lunged at the bassinet to retrieve my daughter before one of these drunks attempted to touch her. I was so incredibly tired, and dealing with
98

them was already more exhausting. "No, thank you. I am actually pretty tired and need to get back to sleep. Thanks for dropping Josh off though." I said with a short and strong tone. The strange lady got the hint and left. I had never been so irritated. Josh always seemed to ruin special moments with his drinking habit.

I attempted to explain to Josh why I was upset and why my feelings were hurt, but he was too drunk to comprehend. It was useless talking to him. It was like talking to a pet rock! He curled up on the chair in the corner of the room and passed out. I fell asleep staring at my baby girl, trying to sooth my deep fear that Josh and I may not work out. This baby was nothing but innocent and pure and Josh's behavior was the complete opposite.

The next morning I woke up to the nurse bringing in a tray of oatmeal and juice that reminded me of the breakfasts I was served at school. I was ravishingly hungry, more so than I had realized. It was nice to have the freedom to eat as much as I wanted without having to worry about it coming back up.

Chloe had been a perfect angel throughout the night. She woke only twice to a dirty diaper, which was extremely awkward to handle. Her little legs were so tiny that it was borderline scary trying to change her diaper. I was afraid of hurting her. The first time around, to my luck, the nurse came in to check my vitals. She must have noticed that I was struggling because she graciously stepped in, in an attempt to show me that changing a newborns diaper was more of a mind-over-matter issue. The second time around was still scary, but I managed to get it done. Josh, of course, was no help as he was lost in his drunken slumber.

It was about eight-thirty in the morning and, to my luck, the mean nurse from my school walked in. Nurse Val. I put on my fake smile and greeted her as I usually did. "Congratulations." She said, practically speaking through her nose. "Are you going to breastfeed?" She was so damn nosey all the time and I really did not want to deal with her at the moment.

"Thanks, and yes, I plan to nurse her." I replied, emphasizing the word "nurse". I was so sick of terms involving anatomy that were spoken so medically correct. It was annoying, and I just wanted my world to be back to normal. As normal as it could possibly be, with a new baby, anyway.

Nurse Val asked me to show her how I would nurse Chloe, while she sat on the edge of my bed. I thought it was odd and totally uncomfortable, but I agreed. She was trying to make sure I had the technique correct, but I couldn't possibly focus on technique when a woman in her forties, that was not even close to me, was staring at my boob! After dealing with Nurse Val for half an hour, she finally left me in peace. Thank God that's over. I thought to myself. At that point I was ready to go home. I wanted my own bed, my own jammies, and my own space. I wanted to bring my baby home for the first time, get her settled and, just maybe, get back into some sort of normal routine.

The only problem I had to face at that point was Josh. If he thought getting wasted on the night of his daughter's birth was okay, he would surely be getting wasted whenever he wanted, from that point forward, without a second thought.

"Josh!" I demanded his attention, not caring that as he was hung-over and looking pathetic in the corner of the hospital room. He looked my way, confirming that I had his attention. "Choose: It's Chloe and I, or alcohol. I am not fucking kidding. You haven't even spent any time with us and I just gave birth to your baby! If you refuse to stay sober, we are done. It's over. So pick. I want an answer now."

I was worried about making Josh choose between me and the booze, but it had to be done. I was scared of what his answer was going to be. I really did not want to do this alone. I knew that I could not do this alone. I wanted Josh to be in our lives forever, but the excessive drinking just had to stop. There was no question in my mind.

To my surprise, Josh got out of the chair with a concerned look on his face. For the first time, he actually looked as if he felt bad for what he had done. Walking to the side of the bed, he grabbed my hand and apologized. "Sweetie, I am really sorry. I am an idiot and I don't know what I was thinking," he said with a voice full of regret. "I don't ever want to lose you. I love you so much and I love our beautiful daughter too." "Well, Josh, you're on thin ice. I am really getting frustrated with your crap and I don't know what to do anymore." I said, trying not to display the ounce of empathy I had left for him.

Out of nowhere, I heard a startling explosion.

Chapter 14

Josh and I simultaneously turned our heads to the corner of the room. Chloe began screaming. I think the explosion startled her too. This explosion was coming from the corner of the hospital room. It was Chloe; her very first dirty diaper. With no further discussion of Josh being in the dog house, we knew we must act quickly. Chloe had been so quiet throughout our stay. Suddenly, she was screaming and I didn't know what to do. She was so incredibly tiny that it was scary changing her diaper. I was scared that any wrong movement would damage her for life. I looked at Josh with total uncertainty "Josh, just go get the nurse because I don't know what to do." I pleaded. Josh's face formed a crooked grin as if he were truly proud of what his baby girl had just accomplished. "Sweetie, I'll change her, it's no big deal." he stated.

As confident as ever, he took charge and changed the green mess like he knew exactly what he was doing. Great. How am I supposed to be mad at him now? Our newborn baby would depend completely on us to give her a safe environment to live in, that was free of alcohol and fighting. However, Josh had done nothing to prove his intentions were to grow up and stop drinking. On the other hand, if Josh and I did not stay together, I would be forced to do most of this teen parenting stuff on my own. I would have to live at my mother's house until I turned eighteen, and even though things at home were great for the time being, I knew they could quickly change back to catfights and bickering to no end. After a thirty second battle with my own mind, I decided to stick it out and see if he was capable of growing up any further. After all, he had just made a small amount of progress.

The clock was nearing noon, and I was ready to spend time at home with my new baby. I was excited when my mother returned from the nurse's station with the news that I could go home. Josh and my mom helped pack everything up, and Chloe was safely tucked into her car seat and ready to go on her first car ride. I could not believe how tiny she looked in her seat. She was so delicate, and every movement with her was slowly and cautiously carried out. On the way home, my mom needed to stop by our local grocery store to grab a prescription for me, and dinner for the rest of us. I thought it would be fun to take my new baby into the store with me and show her off to the envious women who were past their childbearing years. I thought young mothers were so much better than older mothers. At least we were pretty, and still youthful, with enough energy to play with our kids. This parenting thing is going to work out just fine, I was thinking to myself as my mom and I were checking out at the store. The clerk, who had interacted with our family frequently, from several years of our local shopping, was looking at me strangely. She looked confused. Finally, after purposely stepping away from the counter to give her a good look at my new prize, she said "Oh my! How old is the baby? I was hoping it was one of those fake plastic babies the kids all get from school! I'm sad to see that it's not a school assignment!" This ticked me off, and I felt the blood rushing to my face in anger. I gave her no reply. What would I say anyway? "I'm sorry I had a baby." or "Yep, my baby is real!" Luckily, my mother did the talking and I got out of explaining my situation. I was sad after the encounter, because I knew that the negative remark would not be the last one I heard.

We pulled into the driveway of our home, eager to carry our new family member in and get her acquainted. As I began to climb the stairs, I noticed that there were scattered garments laying around. I knew that this was an indicator that Josh had made another horrible mess. He was notorious for this. I walked into my bedroom and was immediately pissed, once again. It was one thing for him to get wasted the night that our daughter was born, but it was a whole different playing field to mess up my personal space. I was livid. I screamed at him from the top of the staircase, and told him that he needed to watch the baby so I could clean up his disgusting mess. He obediently complied.

Still recovering from the strenuous process of childbirth, I was on my hands and knees wiping the dirt off of the bathroom floor. I gathered all of the trash he had left lying around, and finally was able to vacuum. When I was finished getting my bedroom back to normal, I was tortured with painful cramping, followed by gushing blood running down my legs, ruining my new pajama pants that my mom had gotten me just for my recovery. I wanted to have a meltdown, but I was too tired to battle with my OCD any longer. Josh brought Chloe back up to me as I crawled into bed, exhausted. "I wanted to come back and clean up before you came home, I just forgot." He said, with worry in his voice. "Whatever, Josh. Just have some respect in the future. I just had a baby. You never consider important things like that."

I was happy when Josh finally quit babbling apologies and left me alone. By this point, I had learned to tune his uncontrollable rambling out.

He had a true case of ADHD, and his most obvious symptom was speaking nonsense for hours on end. Sometimes he just didn't make sense. I was the one in control, and as long as Josh did as I asked, I truly did not care if he made sense. I did, however, frequently get comments from our peers regarding his conversation style. I knew where people were coming from, but I chose to disregard their input. Josh had good intentions; he was a hard worker, and a nice person. As long as he didn't embarrass me in front of important people, I could deal with it. Josh wasn't crazy, just often confused.

The first night home from the hospital with my baby wasn't the easiest. Chloe took four days to learn how to nurse properly, and this meant that I was waking up every few hours when she became frustrated and hungry. After finally getting the hang of it, on both of our ends, caring for my baby quickly became more of a pleasure than work. Chloe was a very calm and content baby. She hardly cried, and when she did it was always for a feeding or diaper change. Our routine became natural and perfect. That is, as long as Josh was behaving. He had a few nights of trouble, but for the most part, he was on track.

Chapter 15

My mom and I were counting the days to my sixteenth birthday as she was driving me home from my last day of summer school. I wanted to graduate early, so I had hauled Chloe along, and raced through my required courses. As the summer nights passed, our home felt smaller and smaller, with our new addition taking up more room. Josh also had a new addition of his own. His best friend, James, was devastated about having to leave Tahoe when his parents moved out-of-state for a new job. I hadn't really seen much of James during my pregnancy, but once Chloe was born and I was more mobile and motivated to get out of the house. The boys became best friends all over again, and James pretty much became a part of the family. We had a spare room in our home, and both Josh and I thought it would be fun to have James around permanently. We offered him the room with my mother's hesitant permission. He gladly accepted and moved in.

Not long after James moved in, I could tell that my mom was getting tired of putting up with a house full of kids. She wanted, and needed, her own space back. She asked us what our long-term plans were. Josh and I looked at each other and gave her a shrug.

She brought up the marriage topic, again. I thought it sounded fun, and Josh was on board as well. Legally, because of my age, I could not move out of my mother's house to live with Josh unless I married him. With the marriage, I would be emancipated. That meant freedom! Plus, I was really beginning to feel like a loser, with a baby, living under my mother's roof. I knew that I wouldn't have any sort of respect from the community if I remained just another statistic. Josh and I began casually talking about getting married, and the more we spoke of it, the more excited we became. We decided to get married as soon as good ole' Uncle Sam approved: The day after I turned sixteen!

We realized that we only had six weeks until I would legally be permitted to marry in the state of Nevada, which was a short five miles away. After looking through a calendar, we decided on the official date. It would be the day after my birthday, which landed on a Saturday. It was going to be just perfect. But first, we had to start planning and inviting. Unlike my baby shower, I was eager to come up with a guest list and send the invitations out. It was the perfect summer to plan a wedding. It would also be the perfect opportunity to prove to my peers and family members that I was actually kicking ass at the whole teen mom thing.

The first person I wanted to invite and possibly have stand in the ceremony as a bridesmaid, was Megan. When I was pregnant, she ended up moving away to stay with her mom for the remainder of the school year. It was about four hours away, and I had gotten used to her coming and going. She loved living with her dad, Neil, but just needed some time away from him. For the most part, he was a good guy with good intentions. Because he was six-foot-four and clearly just had too much testosterone pumping through his veins; he was easily angered, and I mean fast. There was a summer where Megan and I were considerably bored out of our minds most days. Neil didn't know what to do with us, but I think the fact that I had pretty much moved in for a few months to stay occupied, had made it easier on him to keep his daughter occupied. There were a particular few days that summer where Neil was unusually angry, and getting upset over any little thing that went wrong. Megan's long-lost great-aunt stopped by for a surprise reunion. This put Neil into a state of rage, but he was forced to contain it because he was obligated to be nice to his aunt. This woman really must have had ESP. She came at the perfect time; just as Megan was considering moving back to her mother's home. When Neil had to run to work, unexpectedly, his aunt pulled a white tackle-style box out of her bag. She began to present us with small tablets to use as a remedy for Neil's violent outbursts. She reassured us that the tablets would dissolve immediately, so Neil would not know.

We spent the remainder of our summer drugging Megan's dad with holistic remedies by putting it into home-made Kool-Aid. We loved studying the effects and his response, to know if he needed his dosage upped. It gave us both a sick pleasure to know that we had more control than he knew. He was so easy to trick. This, however, was by far one of the less sneaky antics we had gotten into in our early teens.

I could easily write an entire novel covering our rebellious shenanigans, especially the ones we put over on Neil. The selling point of this novel would most definitely be the incident where we had a naked man hiding in the attic crawl-space of my sister's apartment. Neil came to check on us while we were babysitting and this, of course, was a good judgment call on his end. When we heard him coming up the staircase to the front door, Megan's victim for the night, Marcus, bolted out of the spare bedroom so

111

fast that it took a second for his nudity to register in my brain. He clambered into my sister's closet, knocking things off the shelves, and pulled himself up into the crawl space. I wondered about what the itchy insulation was doing to his naked body. Trying to keep myself from laughing was excruciating.

I called Megan to ask for her address so I could get her invitation mailed. She excitedly announced "Guess what!? I am coming back for good in two weeks!"

Relieved, I responded "Good! Now you can be in my wedding! And Josh has a friend that we both think you should meet. He started renting the extra bedroom a few weeks ago. He decided to not move out of state with his family".

"Oooh!" She squealed with delight. "Is he cute!?" She pried.

"I think he is pretty cute. I really think you will like him. Our boyfriends will be best friends, and we are best friends, so it is just perfect!" I plotted. We ended the conversation in an excited fashion. I was so thrilled to start living a life with friends again. It wouldn't be the same as it had once been, but maybe that was a good thing.

Once again, I put together a guest list, drawing off of the baby shower guest list, except with much more confidence this time. I already knew who my bridesmaids would be, I just had to get enough men who didn't appear to be twelve years old to balance it out. This was going to be an exciting summer.

As promised, a few weeks later, Megan was on her way home. I forced her and James to speak on the phone for a few minutes every time I talked to her, just to find out if they would even like each other. I figured that they must. Opposites usually attract, and their personalities were like night and day. James was pretty calm and laid back. He was a little bit on the passive-aggressive side, but only got mad at me one time when my bath tub water was leaking through the upstairs pipes and onto his bed. He acted like I did it on purpose! It isn't my fault that Chloe and I loved to splash! Megan was not quiet or easy-going at all. She was loud, exciting, obnoxious, snotty, and a complete blast to be around. We could say or do anything, literally anything, in front of each other and laugh about it. The most fun we had was usually laughing over some sort of torturous prank we were inflicting on someone. Megan and I had fun together every day, up until an unspeakable tragedy occurred a few years later.

Chapter 16

Four other girls were to be in my wedding; the first was Mal, (obviously,) then Kate, Holly, and Jessica who had been best friends with Mal since we were eight. Holly had almost been our step-sister at one point. Our parents dated for about a year, and our young families were like the freaking Brady Bunch. We had a blast going to Disneyland in a humungous suburban, torturing the other drivers because we were in love with the Hanson Brothers, and were blasting *Mmm...bop* down the freeway. That really makes me cringe. The Hanson Brothers!? Ugh.

Holly was not only a friend growing up, but she was also like a mediator for twins, and a loving sister trying to keep the peace. She made it hard for me to hold on to grudges. She always laughed at me, or said some hilarious nonsense statement. After inviting Holly to be a part of my wedding, she secretly and cautiously whispered over the phone to me that she was pregnant. "Shut up! NO WAY! Holy shit!" I was throwing the poor girl shocking reactions, instead of advice. I knew she wouldn't mind though. The only problem was that the dress I wanted her to wear for my ceremony was surely going to reveal her pregnancy. I felt her pain; her father was coming to the wedding. We agreed that she should wait to tell him out of fear that he wouldn't allow her to be part of the wedding.

Once the guest list was settled and we had found just enough men to stand in, I was relieved that I was still important to other people. My mother and I spent several days, without rest, planning out all of the details. It was really fun doing this with her. I knew that I could always trust that she had the best taste and class when it came to decisions for me. She knew who her little girl was, and she chose the most beautiful dress for me. The first time trying it on was discouraging. My boobs were implant-huge from nursing Chloe, who was only about six weeks old at the time. My mid-section had some serious flab to lose, and my stretch marks were horrendous. We also went cake tasting, which was a blast. I had a strange craving for lemon that entire summer. I chose lemon icing for the cake and obsessed over lemonade on a daily basis.

We searched the town for a location that would be a happy-medium; not too fancy, but not dumpy either. One of our favorite restaurants at the time was a place connected to the tiny local airport. We would swing by there for lunch often, and the Cajun grit cakes were fantastic. After picking up our engraved champagne glasses (to be filled with bubbly cider, of course) we stopped for our usual gumbo and grit-cakes, and it clicked. This would be the reception location! It was big and bright inside, with huge windows facing the airport runway and the beautiful meadow beyond it. The owner offered to reserve the space and cater a buffet for an extremely reasonable price. On top of my mother's class and savvy, resourceful talent, Pastor Gene offered to, once again, help

116

out. He pitched in a couple thousand dollars, I believe. I still don't know how my mother did it, but she truly planned the most elegant and beautiful wedding a sixteen-year-old could ever want. With the details were taken care of, it was time for the countdown.

Almost forgetting that we wanted to invite Derrick and Donnie, (Josh's co-workers) we stopped by their house last minute to deliver an invitation and show off our little Chloe. Hesitantly walking into a typical bachelor pad with barking dogs, Derrick greeted us with extra positive energy. I set Chloe on a stool in her carrier so I could sit down while the guys talked about nonsense. Derrick looked my way and asked me how I was recovering. "I am doing pretty good, still waiting for my fat to go away, but other than that, I'm good!" I was surprised that he was taking an interest in something that wasn't leading up to a flirtatious remark. Who was I kidding... he couldn't help himself. "Did you get that weird line down your stomach from bein' pregnant?" He curiously and oddly inquired. "Yeah, I got it a little bit, but I think it will fade" I said. "Well, lemme see!" He politely demanded. "Uh...o...kay..." I responded, as I hesitantly lifted my shirt to just above my belly-button. "Aww nah, that ain't shit. You're all good!" He enthusiastically said. I was definitely having a flashback of that horrible mistake I made while we had been fishing last summer. I thought it was strange of him to be interested in the progress of my returning figure. We grabbed our precious cargo and said our goodbyes. It was time to get home to call Megan and have her hurry over. She had just gotten into town, and I couldn't wait to see her.

James was home, being lazy on his bed and babysitting Mal's snake, which we kept far away from baby Chloe at all times. I thought it was so creepy how it strangled its dinner and swallowed

117

it whole, only to crap out bones, which seemed like it would hurt! When Megan's dad dropped her off for the night, I ran to the front door excited and screaming. She looked pretty, as usual, and was still her snotty and sarcastic self. "It's time to meet James!" I sang, dragging her down the hallway, practically launching her into his room. Immediately, the awkwardness kicked in and both of their faces turned bright red, instantly. They eased their way over to each other for a shy hug. It was only a matter of minutes before Megan was bossing James around, and he clearly didn't mind. Megan came over to the couch as I was nursing Chloe to sleep. She was all googly-eyed and giving me the puppy dog face. She had that all-too-familiar mischievous twinkle in her eye. *Oh crap,* I thought, *Megan has an idea. This is bad. This is very, very bad.*

Chapter 17

"What, Megan?" I asked her, with a smirk on my face. "This is so much fun!" she loudly whispered. "You freaking love James, don't you?" I accused. "Sort of!" she giggled. I knew that this was not the only thing on her mind. I didn't want to pry too deep into it with the boys only in the next room. Plus, I knew that we would have plenty to talk about later.

The wedding was inching closer, every day; it was only a week away! My mom picked up a full-time summer position at a local golf course. Josh, James, Megan, and I would frequently visit during her lunch break. They served good food and it was nice getting out of the house. By this time, Megan and James had fallen in love, as I had predicted. It was cute seeing them together, and it was good for Josh and I to have another couple to hang out with who loved being with our daughter as much as we did.

"Lizzy-Beth…" my mother reminded, "You and Josh need to go to Carson City today to pick up your rings. Here is the money, and make sure you get it done because it's right around the corner!" Lizzy-Beth was one of the nicknames that only a few select family members called me. I didn't mind. The only name I did not like was "Liz" or "lizard". They were so unfeminine, and I just hated it. Because I was a teenager and, of course, didn't understand the value or concept of earning money, I excitedly and willingly took the bundle of cash from her. In the back of my mind, however, I did understand that she had been working pretty hard for that money. The singles and fives were evidence of tips. Tips usually signify hard work. I was lucky to have her.

James and Megan decided to go on a *romantic* drive around the lake after lunch, and Josh and I headed down the mountain to Carson City. Tahoe was a small town, and any real shopping had to be done off the hill. No matter how many times we made it, the thirty minute drive was always stunningly gorgeous. There is nothing that can be compared to driving through the Sierra-Nevada Mountains. I highly recommend it.

Pulling into the JC Penny parking lot, Josh got Chloe's carrier out of the back seat and we excitedly walked into the department store. Three weeks previously, I had decided which ring that I wanted to be mine. Peering through the glass, I had instantly spotted my bling. It was only a couple hundred dollars, but it was white gold and it had a touch of diamonds. Josh picked out his ring after trying several sizes on. They were boxed up, paid for, and we were ready to go grab some burgers. Snapping my seatbelt on before the car even started, I was surprised that Josh wasn't eagerly burning rubber as he usually did. He looked at me with a stupid grin on his face. "What are you googling at, weirdo?" I teased. He pulled the box out of the small plastic bag and held it up to my face. "Sweetie, will you marry me?" he asked. "Josh, you are such a dork, but of course I'll marry you!" I laughed. He gave me a quick peck and we were off to chow down. It certainly wasn't the proposal of my dreams, but I guess it was better than nothing.

After we stuffed ourselves mercilessly with lunch, we drove back up the summit as I was played my favorite country tunes. Chloe was totally content, as usual. When we got home we noticed that James and Megan were already home from their drive. We unloaded our precious baby cargo for the hundredth time, and walked in the house, excited to show off our rings. James had his door closed, and my mother was nowhere around. I heard an odd squeaking sound. *Oh my gawd, they're doing it!!* I thought. I knew it was going to happen eventually, but it was awkward that it was in a bedroom in my family's home. At least Josh and I had always been very discreet about it. We decided to wait upstairs in my bedroom until they were done. Finally, when I heard the downstairs door open, I knew that it was safe to resume downstairs activities.

Megan was in the bathroom, fixing her hair. It was a wreck! "Holy crap, what happened to you!?" I questioned. "Hehe, nothin'." She giggled, slyly. "Oh PLEASE! I'm not dumb! Look at the beautiful product of my dumbness." I said, pointing to Chloe. "I know! She is so adorable too!" Megan said in a squeaky baby-talk voice. "Oh no! I know what you're thinking! You have baby fever! Don't you!?" I accused. "Hehehe. Nooooo! Well, just a little bit. Wouldn't we have the cutest little baby?" she affirmed.

After this conversation, I got the gist of where her thoughts were headed. She saw how easy it was to care for Chloe, (who was an exceptionally easy baby) and assumed that it would be just as perfect for her. However, I was somewhat excited about her statement. It would be super awesome to have a friend (my best friend) who had a baby too. That way, we would always be on the same page, and we would have plenty more to talk about. *Our babies would be best friends too!* I was thinking.

123

"Well, if you want what I think you want, I have some things you can have." I offered, as I led her up the staircase. Josh and James were out back smoking their cancer sticks (which I hated). From under my bed, I pulled out a folder and handed her the stack of papers in it. "What the hell is all this!?" She shockingly asked. "Go through it. You'll see" I claimed.

Upon opening the folder, her eyes grew big and her smile was ear-to-ear. "You did it on purpose? I knew it! I don't know why, but I knew it!" I replied with nothing but a shoulder shrug. She read through my once-obsessive material as I changed Chloe. It was official. Without James knowing, she was going to attempt to get knocked up. We talked about it every day after this secret conversation, of course hiding it from the boys.

My sixteenth Birthday had finally come, and the wedding was less than twenty-four hours away. To celebrate our birthday, Mal and I had several friends and family (even from out of town) show up at our home with gifts. My uncle and grandparents brought me a brand new queen sized bed. I was so excited, because Josh was way too tall to share my twin sized bed with me. Also, it was lame sleeping separately even though we had a baby together. After setting up our new bed, my uncle and grandparents announced that it was almost time to head down the street to the church where we would be doing our rehearsal. Luckily, the whole wedding party was there, and everything would go as planned.

Pastor Gene would be the one to marry us, and I was really happy about this. He came up with a great idea of also doing a baptism for the three of us after the vows were completed. I wanted to be baptized. I already felt guilty enough for being so rebellious and reckless at such a young age, and the Good Lord knows Josh needed it too. Standing in the church, near a set of pews, a fly was
124

harassing me as Pastor Gene was going over what his words would be the next day. The fly landed in just the right spot for me to give it a good crunch. I swiftly, like Jackie Chan, stomped on it with my foot, not realizing that I should not have made such a ruckus in a beautiful and calm church. The stomp echoed, and I truly looked like an idiot with Tourette's syndrome, or something. "Liz!" my mom quietly growled. "I am so sorry! I just didn't think! It was a really annoying fly!" I defended.

The pastor finished his beautiful vow compilation, we all shared pizza and cake, and the day was over. The next day was going to be one of the biggest days of my life. I wouldn't let myself think about all of the details; I was already far too overwhelmed. Going to sleep for the first time with my husband and our baby girl, in a big, fluffy and comfy bed was absolute bliss. I finally felt like we were on our way to becoming a normal family. We just needed to find our own place. As I was dozing off, I was fantasizing about what our married life would be like. I pictured Josh and I growing old together, but wondered if he would even live long enough to grow old. He was just so reckless when he was drinking. It had slowed down a little bit for now, but I knew it would come back. I just hoped that I would somehow find a way to help him make a permanent change. Chloe was cuddled up between us, and I was blissfully uneasy.

Chapter 18

I woke up to my sister, Lilah, frantically banging on my bedroom door. "Liz! Oh my gawd! You aren't up yet? The wedding is in an hour!" She was a notorious nag. It drove me crazy. I was just so comfy in my bed. As I slowly inched my way out of bed, Josh opened his eyes and did his usual ADHD pounce to the bathroom to get ready. We were actually going to have two weddings that day. The first one was just to make it legal, and the second would be a bigger ceremony with family and friends. Nevada made it legal to marry at sixteen with a parent's permission. The Officiate that my mother hired would meet us for the legal part at ten-thirty. I honestly didn't even know exactly where it would be, but I hoped it wouldn't be awkward to just have a few important family members there to witness.

When Josh was done showering, he quickly got dressed and grabbed his bag of clothes that he would be wearing for the wedding. He gave me a quick peck on the cheek and raced down the stairs to have James help him get ready so I could have my space. The second I stepped out of the bathroom after showering I was hurried down the stairs by my mother and sister, out of fear that I would be late to my own wedding. I am always late! I was born that way. It actually took my mom an hour and nine minutes to get me, twin "B", out. Usually that sort of thing only takes a minute or two. I take my time with everything, especially important occasions.

I felt like a queen being pampered. My mother, also an aesthetician, was doing my makeup, and my older sister was incorporating beautiful tiny flowers into my long hair. When my hair and makeup was finished, I looked in the mirror and was very pleased. Next, I had to quickly strip down to my underwear so they could tightly wrap a corset around my abdomen and chest. It was perfect for squeezing in the extra baby flab. I called it my flat tire. I stepped into my poufy slip, and then eased my way into my strapless dress. I did not remember my dress looking so beautiful when I tried it on a few weeks earlier. Finally, I was ready. I looked at my reflection in the full-body mirror in my mother's room, and I truly felt like royalty. I had never felt so beautiful in my life. This completely erased any worry or doubt that had been lingering in my insecure mind.

My mother and Mal, along with Megan and the other girls who were still too young to drive, all rode together to the destination. James and Josh rode together, and I rode with Lilah in her truck. My dress was poufy on the bottom, like Cinderella. There was no way I could have sat in a car with other people without causing some sort of damage to the dress.

The drive felt like it was taking forever. It was a bright, beautiful, sunny day which meant that the highway would be full of tourists making their way to the casinos and the beaches. It wasn't anything new, though. Passing the strip of casinos, I knew that we were almost there. We pulled into a local recreational area and for a minute I thought that my mom was making us get married on a soccer field or something crazy. We parked the truck and Lilah hurried around to the passenger side to help me get out of the car so I wouldn't get dirt on my dress. The small group of friends and family were walking at a distance, toward the official spot. I assumed it was safe to follow.

As Lilah and I neared the crowd, I began to see how beautiful the location actually was. I walked up a small grassy hill, and looked around at the surroundings suddenly offered to me; a beautiful panorama of the turquoise lake, surrounded by tall mountains in the distance with perfect, yet modest, icings of snow on the very tops. It was like a secret location that had the most beautiful view I had ever seen. The beauty of my home was suddenly able to my anxious and nervous feelings of growing up so fast. It gave me a complete sense of peace and serenity. I knew that I was supposed to be doing this. I knew that every person there loved me and Chloe, and even Josh. I felt as if I was in heaven, and God was standing right behind me.

As Josh was holding my hands and gazing lovingly into my eyes, the minister spoke of our brave choice to bring Chloe into the world. I don't recall word for word, but I do know that it was beautiful. Right as tears were about to ruin my makeup, I felt an intense, horrid, overwhelming itch. It was under my diamond necklace. *Freaking bugs!* The sparkle from my bling must have been the white light to heaven for those little suckers. They are called no-see-ums, and they dig their pointy little noses into your skin, and it's torturously miserable. Trying with all my might to avoid spastically slapping myself on the neck, I was forced to sink into my meditation zone. Towards the end I was able to casually smear the nasty things into my skin, and I was officially the bug-gut bride. It was still a beautiful ceremony regardless of the dilemma. By the time Josh was permitted to kiss his bride, my itchiness had calmed, and I was able to enjoy the best part.

Josh and I held hands as we walked back to the parking lot to race to our next wedding, where EVERYONE would be waiting. My grandparents had been toting Chloe along, but on the way to the car I just had to see her for a minute. I told her that she was my "little princess" and that I loved her so very much. She gave me a little split-second smile, and I knew that she was aware of the joy. Chloe was a quiet and reserved baby, but she was always aware of her surroundings. The drive back into town had a celebratory vibe. As Lilah and I pulled into the full-to-the-max parking lot of the church, I was extremely horrified. I was scared shitless of the fact that Josh's entire family, from all over the state, and even their friends, were going to be sitting in that church watching ME.

I stepped out of Lilah's truck and told her that I would be right in, and I just needed to talk to Megan for a minute. Megan and James pulled into the parking lot at the perfect time. I knew that they were carrying the goods. "Thank God I found you before you went in!" I frantically said to Megan. James locked his car and announced that he was going to go in to see if Josh needed help with anything. "Where is my promised present Megan?" I begged. "Dude! There are so many people here!" she replied, with wide eyes. She dug to the bottom of her purse and pulled out a small bottle of Bacardi. I crouched down next to the car, looking like a freak in my wedding dress and took two good swigs. There was no way I was going to be able to get through this without fainting, unless I had a few drops of liquid courage. It was just the right amount.

130

Five minutes later I was in the lobby of the church, hearing the quiet chatter of the guests. One of my mother's good friends that I had known since I was five, Lena, was kind enough to bring me a gorgeous bouquet of flowers to carry down the aisle. Before I knew it, I was alone with my uncle, waiting for the music to start. Forgetting the bouquet, and hurriedly grabbed onto his arm. I am sure I had a look of pure terror on my face. He clearly realized how frazzled I was. At six feet, four inches tall, wearing cowboy boots, he smiled down at me. Immediately before stepping into the church, he said something that I'll never forget, but certainly didn't expect; "Ah man, I have the worst wedgie! Great timing." I nearly screeched with laughter. I managed to get a grip on myself in time to avoid looking looney though.

For the second time that day, I met Josh in the presence of the minister, Pastor Gene. We held hands and exchanged vows; I was pleased that it was relatively short. It was then time for my mother to hand baby Chloe over to me for our family baptism. I didn't know how the process worked, but as long as Pastor Gene didn't spray a hose of holy water in my face, (which he would have had the merit to) I would be just fine. It became another peaceful and calm moment. It was comforting to hear his words, and know that God forgave me for my sins, as he always would as long as I asked. I needed that. After Chloe came into my life, my view on rebellion and mischief was changed entirely. She proved to me that we are all born completely innocent, and if she grew up to do the same sort of things I had, it would break my heart.

Because Chloe she was still so young at only six weeks, it wasn't always easy to get a smile out of her. Beyond a coincidence, the moment that Pastor Gene sprinkled the holy water on her head, she contently smiled the most beautiful and innocent smile I had ever witnessed. I was so touched and excited that I actually turned around to announce this to my mother, who was sitting just feet away. "She smiled!" I said excitedly, forgetting that I was in a church, partaking in a life-changing ceremony. All I had eyes for, at that moment, was my precious little girl. She now had an even tighter grip on my heart, which I did not think was possible.

After the ceremony, we all went outside to do the traditional marriage photo shoot. I loved taking pictures with my family, who I did not get to see as often as when I was younger. This was the last time I can remember having the entire family, and close family friends together in the same room. Following the photo session, the large crowd piled into their vehicles to drive to the reception.

At the reception I gave a toast to my mother, bawling my eyes out and telling her how much I loved her, and how I would be "so screwed" without her. Normally, the word "screwed" wouldn't be appropriate at a wedding, especially in a toast, but I was only sixteen, so it was to be expected. After eating from the buffet, and some of the guests getting tipsy at the bar, we sliced our gourmet (and mouth-watering) cake, and opened our mounds of gifts. For the budget that my mother was on, and trying to get her mortgage paid on time, she somehow managed to give me the most beautiful wedding ever. She even got us a suite on the lake for the night. Of course, because I was still nursing, Chloe came along. That was just fine. We were exhausted and overjoyed all at the same time, and definitely looking forward to having a peaceful, relaxing night.

The next day Josh and I were eager to get back home and go through all of our gifts. I was also eager to study for my driving test. I knew that with a baby I would no longer be able to walk to school, especially in the harsh winter conditions.

Settled back in at home, we enjoyed re-decorating my bedroom to look more like a married couples' bedroom. We had a great time obsessing over the wedding photos that were arriving in small increments. Chloe was growing every day, and Megan and James were happy as ever, cuddling, almost non-stop, in the tiny bedroom downstairs.

About a month before school was going to start back up, Megan and I were joyriding in her car, as usual, and on the hunt for some greasy, super unhealthy food. She mentioned that she was irritated when her period had started a few weeks before. "I really, really want a baby. It would be perfect! I am ᴧo sick of my dad bossing me around. He probably has a GPS in my car." she whined. I was excited. "Yeah, it would be a quicker way to get out of his house. And it would be so much fun, too! But don't listen to me, every baby is different. Just because I got lucky with an easy one doesn't mean you will. You have to make sure that you really want this. You aren't going to be able to go out and party whenever you want. Any time you do anything you will have a baby with you. You'll get no free time to yourself, and a lot of mothers don't get much sleep either. Just sayin'." I sat in silence, thinking about what I had just said.

"Oh I know. I have thought about all of that!" she affirmed. We were going through the drive-through as she ordered James a burger with no onions. After she paid, I decided to have her drive down to my school so she could see what would really happen if she got pregnant. She wouldn't want to go to regular school anymore. The other students would talk too much. As I predicted, she got excited about the school, even the hidden away classrooms down the hill. I knew that she had her mind made up, just like I had mine made up not too long before.

133

Chapter 19

"Whoohoo! I freaking passed! I DID NOT think I was going to pass!" I childishly screamed as I skipped down the line of the Department of Motor Vehicles. "Good job, sweet pea!" my mother said. She was carrying Chloe in her car seat as we walked out of the once-horrifying place that would determine my outward appearance as a responsible teen mother. I was desperate to start my junior year with the convenience of driving myself. I was a married woman and a mother, and I needed to look like it. School was only a week away.

After picking up one of my favorite lunches from a little diner, we arrived back home and the phone was ringing off the hook. I answered in my usual monotone "Hello", and it was Megan. "Elizabeth! Get over here, now!" She was breathing heavily like it was a huge emergency. "What is going on?! Why?" I asked. "Just hurry up!" She screamed and hung up on me. Since I had just gotten my license, I thought it would be fun to take myself across the highway to Megan's house. My mom said that it would be okay to use her car, and she even offered to watch Chloe. I grabbed my purse and excitedly headed out the door, forgetting that my friend sounded like she was dying.

"Let me see it!" I excitedly demanded. She practically threw the thing at me and I was happy the cap was on. "Yep, that is definitely a line. You are totally knocked up!" I announced. Megan was still in shock. We sat on the couch and discussed how she was going to break the news to James, and even more worrisome, her dad. After coming up with ideas, I realized that it had been about an hour and I had to get back to Chloe. Now, she would definitely be my study-buddy at school. I also had to make sure that Josh enrolled in the home-study option at the Teen Parents Program, because his ADHD had interfered with his ability to graduate high school. He was a father now, and he had to have his diploma.

That afternoon, after eating my mother's delicious pasta, and putting Chloe down for her nap, I laid on my bed and started thinking about how sad it was going to be to not have a traditional High School graduation. I was determined to graduate this year, which would be a year early. I knew that I would probably end up not walking down the aisle with all the other students, because the traditional Senior Project was always a requirement for that. Oddly, I still had a vision of myself walking down that grassy aisle on the football field, with my family all gathered, clapping and proudly screaming my name. *Only Pipe dreams*, I thought to myself.

The first day of school had finally arrived. Megan was all set to attend the Teen Parents Program, and her dad was still as pissed as he had been the previous week when she broke the news to him. He put a very tight leash on her and she was restricted with everything that she did. James took the news well, although his parents were upset. They thought that it would be best for the baby

136

if they got married. Megan was begging her dad on a daily basis to sign the paperwork to let her tie the knot. He just wouldn't budge. The morning that I was getting ready to show off my new baby to the girls I had made friends with at school the previous year, an intense blaze of sirens went off. It sounded as if it were just down the street. It made me wonder if Mal was ok, as she had just left for school in her beat up Camaro that she dearly loved so much. After about thirty seconds, I heard even more sirens. It must have been at least three police cars and first responders. Feeling sick to my stomach, I hoped for the best and began to pack up Chloe's diaper bag. On my way out, I met my mother in the driveway as she was pulling in. She had gone to make sure the emergency had nothing to do with Mal. Luckily it wasn't. She did say that it looked like a black car had flipped over onto its roof near the entrance of the Keys. The Keys is a neighborhood on the lake, with beautiful and expensive homes.

"Elizabeth! How are ya?" Mrs. Snow asked as she welcomed me in. I gave her a smile and told her that I was ready to graduate this year. "You still have tons of credits to earn, let's just take it one day at a time, okay?" I hesitantly nodded. In my mind, I was determined to graduate, no matter what the obstacles would be. Mrs. Snow sat at the circular table with the group of girls, including Megan and myself. She got a somber look on her face and asked if anyone had heard about what had happen earlier that morning. "I heard some really loud sirens, but that was about it." I responded. Mrs. Snow took a deep breath before she spoke. "There was a fourteen-year-old girl, I think her name was Melissa, who she was skateboarding to her bus stop. Some guys, heading home from a night at the casinos, were speeding and hit her. She was flown to Sacramento, but they don't think she's gonna make it. So sad..." She looked down. Hearing that was incredibly sad, and it bothered me probably more than anyone else in the room. The rest of my day at school was somber because of this, even with Megan cracking her typical jokes. The poor girl did not survive. I actually hung around the same crowd as her older brother, who was my age. Mal dated him in seventh grade, which mainly consisted of holding hands and a peck on the lips. My heart was aching for him, and his family. When things like this happened in Tahoe, it was usually a big deal, and everyone knew about it. It reminds me of the song, "Everybody dies famous in a small town".

School had been in session for about a month, and I was nose-deep in my books and assignments. Megan was gone, again. She and James had gone to live with James' parents. Megan had taken her father to the courthouse on a day that he was loopy from pain medicine, because he had somehow broken his leg. He signed for her marriage certificate, but the next day decided that he was pissed again and didn't want to consent. He hid the marriage license, only for Megan to hunt it down when he was at work. Josh, Chloe, and I followed James and Megan down the hill to Reno where we met up with James' parents, who had driven in from Utah. If Megan was going to get away from her father to be with James, the marriage had to happen quickly. Megan had a last minute melt-down that almost stopped the wedding, but I convinced her that she had no choice. I had written "Congrats Megan and James!" on the back of their car. I didn't have the official car-friendly paint for this, so I figured that my lipstick tube was good enough. I was bawling my eyes out when it came time to say goodbye.

For the next month or so, Josh and I had a hard time adjusting. We had grown attached to living with our best friends. They had become family, and we were very upset that they were gone. Coming home from a long day at school, I walked into the house with Chloe in my arms; she was about four months old already. Josh was sitting on the couch talking to a man in an Army uniform. It took me by surprise, and I was hopeful that Josh was doing something drastic to get our lives going. The recruiter gave me a friendly smile and shook my hand. He began going over different career options for Josh and all of the benefits that our family would have if he joined. It sounded beyond perfect. The next step would be to take a test in a few weeks to see what he qualified for. After that, we would schedule his date to leave for basic training. Josh became overly excited, probably more for bragging rights. He told every person he knew that he was joining the military. Everyone was excited for him, and I was dreaming up a whole new life in my head. I envisioned a small white house in a safe military neighborhood. I saw myself taking care of babies, yes, BABIES, and being the housewife that I wanted to be. The whole idea was romantic: having a husband in the military who would come home every day in a uniform. It couldn't be more perfect.

Because Chloe was so easy to care for, and Josh was joining the army, I thought to myself: This is the perfect time to have another baby! I want to get pregnant before he leaves so he knows that I won't cheat on him, and he will be able to focus on his training. Looking back, I probably, subconsciously, wanted to get pregnant again to put more pressure on Josh to be more responsible. Although he worked, it just was not enough to support us all. Josh's job only paid him a quarter over minimum wage. If it hadn't been for my mother, we would have been in big trouble, financially. I don't know where we would have lived or how we would have fed ourselves without her. I wanted to give my mother a break so I had been spending a lot of time with Josh at his mother's house. She was happy to see more of Chloe. Plus, after Hilda and her fiancée, Edwardo, retired for the night, Josh and I had sexcapade after sexcapade. We both wanted to get our fill before he left for the Army. His test was only a few days away, and the results would determine our fate. By his lack of concern for protection I, again, assumed that he also wanted another baby.

I was getting ready to leave Hilda's house to go to school. Josh had just left with the recruiter to take his test in a town about two hours away. I was nervous for him, mainly because I knew that his untreated ADHD was the reason he did not graduate High School and I worried that it would affect him during the test. I went about my day staying close to my new cell phone that I had recently bought. Finally, right after I finished my disgusting cafeteria lunch, it rang. It was Josh. "Did you pass? What was your score?" I impatiently asked. In a casual, and not very concerned tone, he replied "No, I was three points off. I can't take it again for another two weeks. Sorry sweetie." I was so upset that I couldn't immediately respond. I was let down, worried, and completely disappointed. The test could not have been that hard. "I guess you will just have to study and try again." I said dryly.

I began to doubt Josh and what he was really planning to accomplish in life. I knew that he had potential, but it didn't seem like he was trying very hard. Another week had passed, and I had resumed staying at my mother's house. Josh went back and forth between houses, as usual. After finishing up my homework one night, I finished Josh's homework too-which he refused to complete. As I was putting both assignments away I started counting back to the day that I had my last period. After realizing

140

that I was four days late I knew that I would have to get a test in the morning. I did not announce this to anyone, not even Josh. It was just a suspicion, and maybe it was stress from school, work, and the whole Army ordeal. Before heading to school the next day, I stopped at the grocery store to purchase a pregnancy test. I wasn't about to steal another one like I had before. I had a baby who depended on me now. I just wasn't that person anymore. Once the test was in my possession and Chloe was buckled into her seat, the anticipation was just too much to handle. I went home and decided that Mrs. Snow would forgive me if I were late to class. Anxiously awaiting the results, I once again stared at myself in the mirror. My reflection was much different than it had been the first time. I had a new appreciation for life, and a new respect for what it really took to be a mother. I was happy with what I saw, and who I had become. I was growing up. Glancing down to the counter, the pink line stared back at me, and told me that Chloe would be a big sister.

Announcing this news did not have nearly the same effect as it had the first time around. Josh was the first to find out, responding with an "I love it when you're pregnant!" and a hug. "So you love me when I'm fat? Cause I could have just gone on a Twinkie diet." I teased. I wasn't sure how I felt about this pregnancy. I was excited, but also nervous. Josh wasn't holding his end of the bargain as much as I had hoped he would. Lilah found out next. I had told her that my period was late, and she excitedly went to purchase me another test, thinking it was my first. I took the test and handed it over, knowing what the results would be. "Yep! You're pregnant!" she said. "Hey, Mom! Liz is pregnant again!" she yelled down the hallway. "Is she really!?" My mom responded. My mom wasn't mad, just surprised.

141

The only questionable reaction I received was from one of my teachers at school. She sort of cringed as if she was thinking *what the hell is wrong with you!?* All in all, I had a good amount of support. This also meant that I would really have to come up with an alternate living arrangement. It would be asking way too much of my mother to support Josh and I with a second baby. My mom was busy with her own life at this point, and I didn't want to hassle her any more. She never implied that we were an annoyance, but it was just time to grow up. Josh and I put ourselves on a waiting list for a low-income apartment complex. They only took thirty percent of your income for rent, regardless of what it was. The wait, however, would be about six months. Our other option was a townhouse community that always looked so clean and cute. It was relatively new and I liked how it was so close to school. We put in our paperwork and got a call a few days later. We had been accepted and told that we could move in right away. The only problem was that it would cost $680 that we didn't have. With Josh's job we were only able pay for diapers and car insurance. My mother had given me her old car when she got herself a new one. My mother had given me everything so far. She paid our first month's rent too.

Chapter 20

Continuing my school work, while suffering through terrible bouts of morning sickness, we were getting ready to move into our little one-bedroom townhouse in a few days.

The holidays were coming up, and there was so much going on all at once. I had been consistent and diligent with, not only racing ahead with my school work, but also altering my handwriting just enough to pull off doing Josh's homework as well. I had finally gotten to his last few assignments when Mrs. Snow announced to me that Josh was all set, and would get his diploma in June with everyone else. She wanted him to wait to get his diploma, because she thought that his hard work deserved to be celebrated with a formal graduation ceremony.

Oh, jeez. You have no idea lady. I thought to myself. As I had expected, Josh avoided the Army recruiter, and did not even attempt to study for the test that he had to retake. As far as he was concerned, those exciting and hopeful days were over.

He seemed happy with working his meager job and getting nowhere. It was hard for me to accept this, and I easily blocked it out of my mind, telling myself that he was still young and would eventually grow up.

Moving day had arrived and it was time to say goodbye to the childhood bedroom that had given me many years of comfort and content. I had many life-changing moments in that room, and had grown from a child, to a teenager, to a mother in that room. Every happy, scary, uncertain, and beautiful day had with me falling asleep in that room. I had spent many evenings staring out of my second story window while the sun went down, just thinking and dreaming of what my life would be like in ten years. From getting into sneaky trouble with my twin after our mother had fallen asleep, to getting into some knockdown fights with her (and her evil bird), I was truly sad to leave, and deep down I knew that this would never be my bedroom again. I turned around, with my arms full of my last straggling belongings, to take a last look, and hoped that it would sink into my memory forever.

Walking into our new home for the first time, I was pleased with the cleanliness, but I was displeased with the smell. It had that musty "apartment" smell. It definitely didn't have the smell I was accustomed to. We immediately began putting things away, knowing that Chloe would determine our schedule. As ten o'clock at night neared, we were just about done. I hadn't realized how many belongings we actually had. We somehow managed to acquire everything that we would need to be independent. My mom peeked in through the front door to check on me and ask if there was anything left that I would need. "No, I think we have everything." I quietly said, trying to hide the fact that I was already homesick. "Aww, Lizzy-Beth, I know you're gonna miss home, but you'll be ok!" she said, and rubbed my head. She almost opened the floodgates once more. I knew that this time I had to be strong and tough it out. I was devastated deep down, although I had wanted this so badly, only a year earlier.

Waking up in our new home the first morning was confusing for a few seconds. I knew where I was, but it didn't register that it was permanent. I had a feeling that any minute I would be back in my old room, and life would be as it always had been. It took a week for me to adjust to my new surroundings. I tried to stay busy by going to school, on time, every day, and I even took an extra college course with Lilah to help ensure that I would graduate early. Not to mention, Lilah was a big chicken and didn't want to face a class titled "Human Sexuality" on her own. I thought it was funny, and it would probably be interesting.

Chloe was nearing ten months old, and my belly had once again blown up on me, and much quicker. I was about five months pregnant, and feeling every little pain that came along with it. Josh started drinking even more, and it did not help that he was friends with a neighbor who was his age and also a drunk. It frustrated me and I wanted him to grow up so desperately. There was a night where I had chest pains so intensely that I had to go to the emergency room. But, of course, Josh was passed out drunk and completely useless. The on-call doctor gave me a cocktail of medications, claiming that I had heartburn. I had a horrible reaction to this and ended up hallucinating in the hospital for the next six hours. I was scared and alone; my own husband didn't even try to sober up to be by my side. This made me wonder what else I would have to worry about in the future.

As school continued, I tried to continue to avoid thinking about what an idiot I had married. I was still on track, and getting very close to completing my last few units to graduate. It was actually going to happen a year early and I was incredibly excited. As Mrs. Snow was going over my completed work, I spoke up and told her what I wanted. "So, my twin sister, Mal, is going to be graduating a year early too, and I thought it would be really cool if I could walk with her down the aisle. What do I need to do to make this happen?" Mrs. Snow looked somewhat surprised that I was so serious about this. "Well, Elizabeth, you would need to do your senior project. It is a lot of work and you will have to get started right away. With you caring for Chloe and your pregnancy, are you sure this is something you want to take on?" she asked, looking concerned. "Absolutely! I really want to make this happen, and I know that I can." I reassured her. It was official. I was going to tackle my senior project and make my vision come to life. Everyone would be proud of me, and more importantly, I would be proud of myself. I was ready to prove to the world that I was more than just a statistic.

After living in our new home for only about two months, Josh and I received a call from the manager at the other complex we were interested in that offered low-income families a realistic solution to paying rent. We had finally reached the top of the list and could move in the next week. I was thrilled knowing that we would have two bedrooms. We managed to break our lease with the townhouse management, and began packing for our next move, right down the highway. I was six months pregnant, and it was perfect timing considering our new addition would be making an entrance soon. As I brought Chloe up the stairs to our new place, I excitedly showed her to her new room. "It's your own room Chloe! Aren't you excited!?" I babbled. She gave me an adorable grin and clapped her hands. Our family unpacked in about two days, and it was exciting to settle into a place that could be more permanent because of the extra space it offered. Our neighbors were all very friendly senior citizens and they were very curious about Chloe and my new pregnancy. They never openly questioned my age, and

I truly felt as if I were an accepted part of their small community. The downside was that Josh knew quite a few people living in the neighboring building. This encouraged his drinking habit even more. It felt like the more pregnant I became, the worse his drinking became. There were several nights when he did not come home until four or five in the morning, if not later. I would stay up and silently cry, wondering if he was okay and wondering if he still even loved me. I could not understand why he felt it was so important to be out, getting wasted, instead of being at home with his wife and daughter, who loved him.

In the classroom of the senior project presentation, I was a nervous wreck. *Who in their right mind does a senior project on soup!?* I asked myself. My mother had been my chosen mentor that was required to work with for the completion of the project. She was a great cook, and we thought it would be fun to experiment with soup and make a cookbook to give to the judges when my presentation was finished. They were all adults, and they were all successful members of the community. Most of them were business owners. They were very friendly to me, despite the fact that I was eight months pregnant. After asking me what my future plans were, I replied "I am going to take college classes full-time to get my degree in nursing. I love to help people and I have always loved the hospital environment." The judges all seemed very impressed with my drive and they were probably surprised that I wasn't another statistic, thus far.

I passed my project with a ninety-five percent, and I was thrilled that it was almost time to live out my vision of having a normal graduation. Ironically, for the graduation ceremony, all of the graduates were instructed to wait down the hill, where I had attended school for the last few years. They would signal to us when it was time to start walking to the football field. I was so pregnant, and so hot, I thought I might faint. Luckily, Mal was right there with me and would most likely make an attempt to catch me if I did. The band started playing the popular graduation song and, in a line, standing next to our walking partner, we started moving. Once the green field came into view, my fears calmed. I began to feel proud of myself, and truly in awe that I had made it this far. Sixteen, married with a baby, and another one on the way, I knew at that point that I was officially not a statistic. With our entire family in the crowd, I knew that I had met my goals and even more. Following Mal, the principle called my name, and shook my hand as I happily accepted my diploma. I had officially graduated High School and could start my life as a young, aspiring adult, who would do great things and one day be an example to other young parents.

Chapter 21

The summer after graduation was hot and miserable. I was ready to pop and desperate to get the baby out. My mom had been spending a lot of time at my apartment, knowing that I needed help with anything she was willing to do.

It was a normal, hot, boring Saturday, and Josh decided to ditch the family and go fishing with Donnie. I honestly didn't care, because he was getting on my nerves anyway. My mom, Chloe and I went on a little shopping spree, and she got me my favorite combination of the pregnancy-preferred sacks that I was currently obsessing over. Once we got home and blasted the fan, I practically fell back onto the couch, ready to chug my soda and indulge in my kit-kat bar. It was already the late afternoon and of course I had no update from my husband or his whereabouts. This was sadly typical behavior to be expected from him. But, as it started to become dark outside, I did begin to become worried and I quickly became angry, knowing that he was probably just too drunk to remember to update me...again. I was extra upset because I was so pregnant and expecting to go into labor at any moment. It hurt my feelings that he just didn't care.

"RING...RING...RING..." My house phone blared. It was nine o'clock at night. I had a bad feeling. Josh typically called me by six, or just showed up the next day. Rarely did I get a peak-party-hour update. Picking up the phone, I could not believe what I heard.

"Hello, is this Elizabeth? My name is Nurse Mary and I am with the Chico State hospital, emergency department. Your husband, Josh, was in a roll-over car accident and flown here because he was periodically going unconscious."

The nurse gave me this information as if it were an everyday conversation. I guess it was, to her.

"Oh my gosh. Okay...Is he going to be alright?" I asked, with a trembling in my voice and my hands shaking as I gripped the phone. "Oh yes! He is doing well now. We are waiting on some simple test results but other than that he should be free to go home tomorrow."

After getting off the phone, and telling my mother what had happened, I was initially in a panic to get to the hospital that was five hours away to be with my husband. My mother was the only one who could take me, because I had no idea where this place was and was too pregnant to go that far on my own. "Honey it's almost ten at night and Josh is fine. We need to wait to get him until the morning Liz. Maybe this will teach him a lesson" she affirmed. She was right, and if no one rushed to his rescue, maybe it would force him to think about it even more. I felt like I was reliving that Thanksgiving night that he went to jail, except I felt a different kind of sympathy. It was an exhausted sympathy that was running out. The one thing that these two incidents had in common was alcohol.

154

The next day we made the long drive to pick up Josh. He looked beat up, hung over. I was glad that he was at least alive. I forced an explanation out of him once we got home. Apparently a tire on Donnie's truck just suddenly "fell off" causing them to flip. That was total crap, and I knew it. I also knew that he would stick to this lie, to protect Donnie. He wouldn't admit that the two of them had been drunk and speeding.

The accident caused Josh to slow down on his drinking for a couple of weeks. It was good timing. I was really pregnant, and really needed him to just grow the hell up.

In a desperate attempt to put my body into labor, I went on five-mile walks with Josh, gagged down castor oil and orange juice, had miserable sessions of sex, and made a pathetic attempt at jumping jacks. This kid was going to come when it was ready, and there was nothing I could do to change it. After taking a long cool shower one hot afternoon, I dried off to realize that my leg continued to stay wet. I dried it again, and it was soaked again. My water was leaking. Happy and nervous, I called my mother to come pick me up, and I called Josh at work, instructing him to head over to the hospital. The nurses admitted me and ran a test to make sure I was correct, and sure enough, one of them announced "Let's put it this way; you aren't leaving this hospital without your baby in your arms."

I let out a sigh of relief. Although I knew that it would never be the same, I wanted my body back. Chloe's birth was painful, but I was confident that I could deliver Zoe without an epidural. I would be induced the next morning at seven. I tossed and turned the whole night in anticipation, with Josh by my side. My mother spent the night so we could be with me in the morning. When Seven o'clock finally rolled around, we were arriving at the hospital. I explained my wishes to the nurse; that I just wanted to go with the flow, and if I ended up needing medicine I would let her know, but I could probably do without. My mom had dropped Chloe off with Hilda, which was a rarity, because Hilda was seldom sober. When she was sober, though, she was a good grandma. Mal was hanging around the hospital room, nervously pacing. She somehow got stuck with my mother and had no way to get home. She wasn't the type to be a part of anything gruesome, involving humans. She helped out with surgeries on animals for her senior project, but that was a different story for her. By ten o'clock the pain was nearly excruciating. The pressure, once again, was overbearingly nauseating. At that point, I couldn't handle any more. "I need the epidural, like now!" I demanded to the nurse. "Well, you are already eight centimeters. I will call the anesthesiologist, but don't get your hopes up because he may not arrive in time." *You have got to be absolutely fucking kidding me.* I angrily thought. I was so disappointed that it was borderline heartbreaking. The memory of the intense pain was all coming back to me, full-force.

Unlike the last time, I was in a full-blown panic, and scared to death of what I knew was to come. I fought it pretty bad. I really wanted no part in this ordeal. Not to mention, the nurse's lack of giving-a-shit really fueled my fire. Mal became so scared of the screams coming out of my mouth, she had to face the wall and plug her ears. I later learned that she was actually in the corner of the hospital room having a full-blown panic attack. "AAAAAAAAH!! Get this thing out of me NOW!" I wailed. I was in so much pain that screaming was the only way to release it. Finally, the Dr. had to get in my face, force me to make eye contact with her, and tell me to push, instead of scream. I came to my senses and understood

156

that she was right. On the next contraction I pushed as hard as I possibly could, and that familiar and beautiful sense of relief overcame me. It was finally over. Our new baby, another girl, was a beautiful little screamer that looked just like her sister. Her face was a little swollen from the quick entrance she made into the world, but she was gorgeous, and I was immediately in love. We had decided that if we had another girl, her name would be Zoe.

After the doctor tested my patience with stitches, and who knows what else, I was finally able to sit in a normal position and hold my baby girl. Visitors came and left, and the night fell. This time, Josh was by my side the entire time. He helped me when I asked, and he said nothing about leaving to go anywhere that surely would have led to alcohol streaming down his throat. For once, I actually felt like we might be okay, and he might have just grown up a little bit. In the middle of the night, Zoe started to cry out of hunger. I was happy to have more confidence than I had had with Chloe. I picked the sweet, little life up from her bassinette and brought her to my chest. "I love you so much little girl. I am so happy you are here and part of our family." I whispered, as I welcomed her cuddly embrace. The most innocent creature to ever greet the planet is, without doubt, a newborn baby. Incredibly innocent and incredibly helpless. Unlike Chloe, Zoe didn't make many creaky door noises. I noticed that she had a frown on her face, and a lightning-fast thought came and left my mind all in an instant. *What if she knows something that we don't? What if she foresees a sad future?* The thought of anything sad happening in my precious little girls' lives hurt my feelings. I quickly erased it and fell asleep with her on my chest.

The next morning my mother brought Chloe into the hospital room as we were getting ready to check out. The sweetest sight

157

that I had ever witnessed, and the most symbolic sight as well, was when Chloe, with assistance, at only fourteen months old, held Zoe on her lap, and became so excited that she laughed out loud. Chloe was thrilled to have her baby sister. It was almost as if she knew that her best friend had finally arrived. They were meant to be in each other's lives, for more reasons than anyone will ever understand.

Bringing Zoe home was a new experience. I was lucky to have my mom's help with Chloe when Josh was working, but without my mom around, it was just me and two babies. It became a blur, and I remember asking myself, at one point, if I could handle it. Physically, I only had so many arms! Mentally, I felt okay, just unsure if I would be able to keep up with the demands. My day was diaper change after diaper change, nursing Zoe, feeding Chloe, battles over nap time, meltdowns over competing for attention. Bed time didn't even provide any relief because I was too nervous to keep them in their own rooms. I would be scared of a variety of scenarios: someone might break in, the house would catch fire, one of them would stop breathing…you name it, I worried about it. Finally, when Zoe had her first birthday, I finally started to feel like I was adjusting to having two babies still in diapers. I had lost most of the baby weight, and I was starting to feel like I had more energy and a better grip on a routine.

I was excited when I learned that Megan would be moving back. Apparently she was sick of Utah, and couldn't stand James' mother bossing her around. I was interested to see how we would go on our joy-rides with three babies in the back seat. In order to be a happy mother I needed to have a routine of getting out of the house once in a while. I was enrolled in community college courses full time, and my goal was to transfer to nursing school after two years. I was a bit nervous when college started, as I hadn't done much socializing in what felt like forever. I managed to get the girls enrolled in daycare part-time, and I had my paperwork turned in for school, and my schedule set. I was approved for financial aid as well, and I knew that would help tremendously.

On my first day of school, I was nervous and sad about dropping the girls off at daycare. I was worried that the girls might flip out and think that I was abandoning them. It was definitely more difficult for me than it was for them. Chloe wandered off, infatuated with the mounds of new toys and other kids, and Zoe had no idea what was going on, but she didn't cry and that is all that mattered at the moment.

My classes were laid back, and after going through each syllabus, I realized that I could easily get through them. The more I did my homework and aced my tests, the more confident I became. I was completely driven and motivated to get into nursing school. I knew that I loved to help people, and I had a way of putting myself into other's shoes. My first round of final exams had come and gone, and, eager as hell to know how I had done, I pulled up my grades online. Three As, and one B I was so excited that I let out the most high-pitched, girly scream that was totally foreign to me. "Sorry...!" I said to Josh as he startled and looked my way, annoyed. I had proven myself wrong once again, and beat the odds. I was a mother, a housewife, and a full-time student and doing all of these tasks exceptionally well. Life couldn't be better. Except for Josh. I knew deep down that if I ever wanted to offer my babies a good life, I was going to have to do the hard work and become independently successful. Josh didn't have the drive that it took, and his drinking problem was getting worse by the day.

Chapter 22

The holidays had come and gone, I was in my second semester of college, and Megan, James, and their daughter, Kylee, had moved into the apartment complex, a few buildings down from us. We were happy to be neighbors, and began hanging out like the old days. It was good for Josh to have a friend that wasn't a raging alcoholic, like he had become. Megan and I managed to squeeze all three of the girls into the back seat of the car any time we wanted to go somewhere. Kylee was between Chloe's and Zoe's ages. It was adorable lining them up from biggest to smallest. We resembled a teenage version of the "Desperate Housewives", no doubt. We were bored with the same stuff happening on a daily basis, and our husbands became boring. We got out of the house and left them together as much as possible.

Eventually, we thought it would be entertaining to find some guys to flirt with. We didn't intend on moving an inch past flirting. One sunny (but icy) afternoon, Megan needed to stop at the tire shop to get a flat repaired. Sure enough, Josh was working his usual shift. Of course, Donnie and Derrick were also working. Donnie instantly started to flirt with Megan. It was obvious that she was entertained by the thirty-two year-old's attention. I assumed that she was just playing along. And go figure, Derrick, who I had written off as a total pervert, was attempting to get any reaction out of me that he possibly could. "So Elizabeth, how should I break up with Macy? She is just too dumb for me. I need someone smart, like you" he said. "I don't know, just tell her she is a total idiot and you never want to see her face again." I said, annoyed. "Daaaamn girl, ouch!" I wanted Derrick to think that I was not a nice person, even though I was. I wanted him to not like me, and to not hit on me. It backfired and made him want me even more. Now I was a challenge to him, and he would be on an intense mission to make me his. "I'm married, with two kids." I pointed to the back seat as he was loitering. He smiled, laughed, and walked away. "Come see me when you're eighteen!" he yelled. This man had no shame! With my husband directly behind us, knowing that Josh wouldn't say anything, he blabbered on. I felt bad for Josh, and I knew that it really took a hit to his self-esteem. On the drive home, I said to Megan, "I don't know... Derrick is cute and everything, but I just have a bad feeling about him that I can't quite pinpoint." "Really? That's weird. I don't think he's that bad."

As the winter months dragged on, Megan and I had a bad case of cabin fever. Eventually, she and Donnie exchanged numbers, as friends. This led to us making secret stops at their house on a daily basis. We never got out of her truck; the guys were beyond happy to come outside and hang on the car doors and chat. Their house was a dump. It was on a dirt road that shared the same property as an abandoned trailer. I later learned that they were growing massive amounts of marijuana in the trailer. Megan and I ditched our husbands when we could get away with it, and snuck to their house as much as we could. I hated Derrick hitting on me like a sick pervert. I subconsciously liked the attention though. Josh didn't know how to make me feel that way. Josh wanted sex and dinner, and that was it. He could never have a serious conversation with me. Our marriage felt childish, and fake. The more he drank, and the more he failed to come home at a decent hour, the more respect I lost for him. Josh was still a boy. By no means was he ready to be a man and really be around to support his family. I was not ready to leave Josh, but it was fun to daydream about other options. Maybe I let myself daydream too much. Each time Josh brought the bottle to his mouth, I fantasized even more about finding a person to be with who could genuinely take care of myself and the girls. I wanted a normal family environment and I was so sick of worrying on a nightly basis weather or not Josh was going to come home, or if I would get a knock on my door from authorities stating that he was dead. If he had ended up joining the Army and dying in combat, at least it would've been an honorable death, and his girls could grow up proud, knowing that their dad died a hero. Dying from the resulting damage of getting behind the wheel wasted, was the absolute opposite of heroic. It was shameful and selfish.

I began to realize that it was becoming more and more unfair for the girls, and myself, to base our lives around his drinking and the stupidity that came along with it. I called a local recovery center to inquire about treatment for Josh. "You can't force your husband to come to treatment, and unless it is court ordered, there is nothing we can do. He needs to come in himself and agree to stay." I sighed and thanked the lady for the information. There is no way in hell he will agree to stay in treatment, I was thinking. It was so easy for me to just want to give up on him. It would be one less thing to worry about if he wasn't in my life. Of course, I would always want him to be a part of Chloe and Zoe's lives, but I was tired of babysitting a now twenty-two year old man. He was clearly not going to grow up any further.

Finally, one night, after Josh had been drinking for eight hours, I just couldn't take it anymore. If you can't beat 'em, join 'em. I gave in, opened a wine cooler, and sat down at the kitchen table to play cards with his friends. I was willing to go to whatever extent it took to either give Josh the wake-up call that he needed, or just get it over with and end the marriage. I caught a buzz and became flirty. I figured this would result in one of two things. Josh would man up and ask his friends to leave so we could have a serious talk, or he would feel sorry for himself like the drunken mess that he had become, and do nothing to help the dilemma. Josh noticed my harmless flirting and embarrassed us both. He sat in the corner and dropped his head, slurring profanities at me, and then caved in to a drunken sob. He couldn't possibly have been aware of what he was doing or saying with how intoxicated he was. *At least Derrick doesn't drink*, I thought. Chloe and Zoe were in bed, asleep, and I knew that if I bolted out of the house before he could catch me, Josh would have no choice but to stay home until I returned. Slightly drunk, in booty-shorts, and feeling much too ballsy, I did just that. Because it was one in the morning, I was really unsure of where exactly I was going. I wanted to go to Derrick's house, and see what would happen if I was a dick tease. But, I didn't think he would be awake.

I slowly drove past his house, and I saw the reflection of the glaring T.V., someone was awake! Thrilled, I pulled in and drove down the bumpy dirt driveway. I assumed that it would be Donnie awake and wasted, which was his usual routine. After knocking on the glass sliding door, Derrick opened the curtains, and with his

164

eyes wide in shock, he smiled and told me to come in. Looking me over, he said "Look at you hottie. What are you doing awake right now, isn't it past your bed time?" I shrugged. "Josh is a total idiot and I just can't stand it anymore. It's just not going to work. He is a full-blown alcoholic, he never helps with the girls when I need to do homework, and it is like having a third child. He just won't grow up!" I ranted. "I knew this all along." he gloated "I knew that one day you wouldn't be able to handle it and you would show up at my house, knocking on the door in the middle of the night" he said with a smirk on his face. I socked him playfully on the arm. As much of a pervert as he was, I was impressed with his ability to hold a serious conversation. He actually had some knowledgeable insight. He was starting to grow on me with each passing minute.

We sat on the couch as he finished watching his movie. It was some sort of boring action movie. Testing the waters, he decided to get complacent as he laid his head on my lap. I put my hand on his head as a green light. Before we knew it, we were making out, with him on top of me on the old, beat up couch. I just wanted to feel like an adult, being loved by an adult. *Now THIS was a man,* I thought, *physically and mentally.* One thing led to another, and it happened. We had sex. I officially cheated on my husband, whom I vowed, in front of God, family, and Chloe, to always be true to. The sign that it was really over, for me, was that I didn't feel bad. I was more excited that I had the chance to see what else was out there, and in my mind, at that moment, Derrick was much more than I thought him to be. I instantly fell in love with him.

After getting busy, it was around four in the morning. We were hungry, and decided to take a drive to get breakfast at the casinos. In my pajamas and pig-tails, I fearlessly, now eighteen, sat down at the wheel-of-fortune game, and tried my luck with a

165

twenty dollar bill that Derrick put in for me. I thought that it was so cool how he could just spare an extra twenty dollars like that. To me, in my world, that was a lot of money that could go pretty far. Lucky me, I won back two-hundred and twenty dollars. I thought that this was an awesome sign, and offered to buy breakfast. After dropping Derrick off at home to get ready for work, I headed over to my mother's house where Josh had dropped the girls off. I was so tired, and feeling hung over. As I was lifelessly lying on my mother's living room floor, Josh knocked on the door. I had nothing to say to him. I began to feel guilty, and it was too much to handle. I just ignored him. "Elizabeth. I know what you did last night." he accused. "This is your last chance to talk to me, because I have someone else who will treat me better and wants me." I still did not respond, though adrenaline was pumping through my veins. I had a feeling that I knew who he was referring to. It was a fifteen year old girl named Alena, who Megan had been hanging around with, out of pity for her screwed-up family life.

As soon as Josh left, I called Megan and demanded to know what was going on. To my surprise, Alena answered the phone. "What do you want, you stupid whore? Oh, and by the way, your kids are ugly. My baby is way prettier" She childishly sang. "Oh please, little girl. Where is Megan?" I heard Megan scolding Alena for answering the phone. "Dude. What the fuck is going on? Are you hosting a fuckfest for my husband and that little girl, or something?" I demanded of Megan. "Um, nooo." she said, in her snotty tone. "They were flirting earlier today, but nothing serious. Why would you care anyway, aren't you with Derrick now?" she accused. "I don't know what is going on, but regardless, you are supposed to be my friend! I guess I really have no idea who you

166

are!" I screamed, hanging the phone up, with tears streaming down my face. I had a million emotions going on, all at once, and I didn't know how to process them. I went outside and lit up a cigarette. I had not smoked up until then. The nicotine made me happy, and I went down the street and bought a carton.

Later that evening, while battling with Josh over the phone, I was tormented by sex noises coming from the background. I assumed it was to give me unmanageable grief. I was at a loss, and there was no bargaining. There was no way to make it better with Josh. We had both done each other wrong, and the damage was too severe. I had reached to the point of just wanting to go home and work it out for the girls' sake. Josh was not being reasonable, but could not even bite his tongue for one second to let me talk. I could hear Alena and Megan egging him on. I was sad that my best friend had suddenly turned on me, and I really didn't know why. She was the one constantly wanting to go flirt with the brothers, and now she was stabbing me in the back.

I was close to a meltdown until Derrick called me at the end of the day. "What's up? Are you okay?" He genuinely asked. "Not really... just a bunch of drama." I said. "Well, hey, let me buy you dinner tonight. Do you want to go down to Route 395 Grill in Carson?" "Hell, yeah!" I replied. It sounded like heaven getting off the hill and away from all of the mixed emotions. I packed up Chloe and Zoe and picked up Derrick. He was clearly comfortable around me already, talking about work and life at home with his brother, and farting in my car (which I thought was disgusting). I'll never understand why men think it's just fine and dandy to blow ass in front of a person who they barely know, let alone a woman they are interested in. I tried to block it out and focus on safely driving down the windy summit. We arrived at the restaurant, and

167

without hesitation, Derrick got out of his seat and opened the back door where Chloe was sitting. He helped her out and held her hand to cross the street. As I was carrying Zoe, who was about thirteen months old, my heart melted and this made me want Derrick even more. It seemed like he naturally knew what to do, and if I were to have another relationship, that would be necessary in the man I chose.

Chapter 23

Our barbeque dinner was delicious, and sitting with Derrick and my girls felt natural. He took initiative and helped chase down the girls when they began to get bored at the table and stray. He even shared pieces of his dinner with Zoe. Either he had experience with children or it was a big show to melt my heart. And of course it did. "How are you so great with kids? I had no idea you had this side!" I said, teasingly. I squeezed Chloe's adorable two-year-old cheeks "Derrick is so good with widdle ones isn't he?" I said in a baby voice. "Yeah!" Chloe responded. She was my girl, always vouching for mommy. We had dined outside on the patio and, although it was a little chilly, the heat-lamps above us were soothing and romantic. After eating until our stomachs hurt, we had to head back up the hill to get the girls put to sleep. It was getting late, and at that rate they wouldn't be in bed until eleven at night.

I had Derrick drive us back. I hated driving in the dark, and I didn't have my glasses with me. He drove cautiously, and I respected that. Josh always drove wild and free, just like his ADHD. Driving in the dark, the girls passed out, and I started wondering out loud how I would get into my apartment. "Josh somehow stole my only key, and I know for a fact that he isn't going to give it to me." I said. "Just stay away from Megan's apartment." he warned. "You know Josh is there fuckin' that little fifteen-year-old. You're gonna wind up in jail if you don't listen to me." I figured he was probably right, but it was not fair for Josh to take this out on his innocent daughters. They needed their jammies, diapers, and wipes; I had nothing for them to wear over at my mothers' house. It was the whole principle of the matter that bothered me.

After driving for thirty minutes, we pulled into Derrick's driveway so I could switch places and get the girls to bed. When I got out of the car, he met me at the hood and grabbed me by the waist. Quietly, he whispered, "Girl, don't make me fall in love with you just to hurt me. If you're gonna hurt me, just get it over with." He lifted my chin and slowly kissed me. It was a long, passionate kiss, one that I had never experienced. It was a true kiss; a kiss that he put his feelings into. "I'm not going to hurt you." I promised. "Trust me, I've made my mind up about how I feel. I wouldn't be throwing my marriage away if I was questioning how I feel about you." He kissed me again. This time, longer, harder, and more passionately than before. He kissed me like he really meant it. I kissed him back even harder. Before it got too out of hand, he gently pushed me away. "Now go get those girls in bed, and don't go to jail or I'll be pissed." He demanded. "Alright, I won't. Call me tomorrow. Okay? And thanks for dinner." I smiled sensually and walked back to my car.

Pulling out of the driveway, I knew it was game time. No guy was going to screw me, or my daughters, by denying us our basic needs. Without thinking twice, I headed straight for my apartment

172

complex, knowing that I was getting that damn key, no matter what it took.

As I pulled into the parking lot, I dialed Josh's cell number. The lights were on in Megan's apartment, and it was obvious that a good time was going on. "What do you want, bitch?" Josh answered. "Josh, I don't want to fight with you. I want to stay civil, and I just need you to let me into the apartment so I can get diapers and clothes for the girls." I pleaded. "Haha, yeah right, you fucking hoe. I'm busy with better things, and a better girl. You ain't gettin' shit!" He slurred. As I had anticipated, he was drunk. No surprise there. I pulled up in front of Megan apartment and turned my brights on. When no one came out, I began flashing them. My adrenaline was pumping full-force. My heart was racing with rage. Alena walked out wearing her fifteen-year-old pig tails and fluffy slippers. She stopped on the grassy hill and put her arms in the air as if she were a gangster from the hood. "Your man would rather fuck a real woman! You don't deserve him. He's mine now, bitch!"

I laughed to myself and came to my senses. If I were to accept her invitation for a fight, I would surely go to jail. I was legally an adult, and she was still an idiotic kid. If I was going to end up in jail, I was going to at least do it with a bang. I had the common courtesy to keep my affair quiet. I knew that making a statement and rubbing it into Josh's face would surely be far too hurtful. As angry as I was, I wouldn't have wished that kind of pain on anyone. Even though we were fighting, and it was over, I still loved Josh. I knew that a part of me always would. He gave me the most beautiful gifts that any person could ever ask for. For that, there will always be a sense of appreciation.

Josh finally walked out of the apartment and down the grassy hill. I knew right away that he would not have the ability to reason

173

with me, especially because he had been drinking. Defeated, and praying for an ounce of empathy, I calmly asked him, "Josh, the girls are sleeping, I just need their things. You don't even have to let me in, will you just get me their things, please?" Almost in tears, I looked him in the eyes. "Nope! You fucked up and I'm not doing shit for you!" he yelled. I made a third attempt, then fourth attempt, and just like the girl I hit with the plastic softball bat, my patience ran dry. Alena came closer to the parking lot, starting the yell. "Josh! Get away from that nasty hoe! Let's finish where we left off, you know, I was going down on you?" This little girl was a terrible instigator. Whether what she was saying was true or not, it cut me like a knife. It cut me deep. Josh looked over at her, "Hang on sweetie, I'll be there in a minute." *Sweetie? SWEETIE! This is the value he places on that word!? The first pet name any man had ever given to me? HELL NO!* I raged, to myself. Completely losing any sense of time or place, I slammed my car into reverse and backed up about five feet. Josh was standing against his car, and I aimed my front bumper right toward him. "Give me the fucking key, you sick piece of shit! Give it to me now!" I screamed. Josh stood there, un-phased. I inched my way toward him, and his precious car, slowly but aggressively.

I was so close he almost didn't have room to make his way out of the metal gap. "I'm giving you a fair warning, Josh! If you don't give me that key RIGHT NOW, I am going to FUCK your car up!" I devilishly yelled. "You're not getting the damn key!" He screamed. He must not have truly known what I was capable of at that moment. Out of his own anger, he kicked my side mirror so hard that it flew off, only hanging by wires. "Go to your mother's house, you stupid bitch!" He violently yelled. "That's it, you stupid, lowlife piece of crap! I gave you a chance, and I warned you!"

Slamming the car into reverse even harder this time, I backed up about ten feet. I sat for a moment, giving him one last chance to hand that key over. When he clearly didn't expect me to do what I had threatened, I released the brake. I gassed the car just enough to make it lurch forward, but not enough to cause a rough impact. I was able to put a nice sized dent in the side of his car, but it just wasn't enough. I wanted his whole car to be completely shattered, just as my feelings were. I backed up again and gave it another whack, a little harder. I still wasn't satisfied, and I knew that I had to get out of there because someone was probably calling the cops. I reversed my car one last time, knowing the last time would be the best. I slammed my front end into his passenger side door, and gave it the damage I was hoping for. When I was finished my heart was pounding and my entire body was numb with adrenaline. I pulled out onto the quiet highway, expecting to be pulled over any moment. I laughed as I saw the police drive right past me and turn into the apartment complex. I was hoping that I would at least make it to my mother's house before being arrested. I had completely forgotten that my sleeping babies were in the back seat of the car. They stayed sleeping and quiet the whole time. Fear rushed through me as I pulled into my mothers' driveway. I had officially been a bad mother than night. I lost my mommy innocence. I royally screwed up, and I fully knew it.

I turned off the car and unbuckled the girls from their seats. When I walked inside, my mom was just getting ready for bed. "What's up, sweet pea?" she asked. "Is everything okay? It's pretty late." The girls heard their Grandma's voice and became alert. They both loved her, and wanted to wake up to play. I was

175

exhausted, mentally and emotionally. I set them down, and took my sweater off from the heat of my boiling blood. "Oh, nothing. I went to dinner then tried to get the key from Josh. He wouldn't give it to me and we got into a really bad fight. He messed up my car, and the cops might be coming." I calmly lied. I didn't want to give her all of the details if the cops didn't show up. I could possibly get away with it. "Well, if he messed up your car, why would the cops come for you?" she questioned. "That's true. You know what? I think I am going to call the cops on him right now." I decidedly announced. "Liz, are you sure it is that bad?" she asked. "Yes. It's that bad." I replied.

I had a great plan: I would call the police on him, and they would have to believe me. I would simply tell them that I thought my car was in reverse when I drove into his car. I was so scared and frazzled from his yelling that I just wanted to get out of there! My plan was going to work like a charm. Fifteen minutes had passed and I was wondering if the police were even going to show up at all. I was able to find some pajamas for the girls in the diaper bag, and get them cozy and ready for bed. I was tired and just wanted to get the police interview over with. My mother was waiting up with me, although she looked exhausted and unsure.

"BANG BANG BANG! It's the police! Open up!" a man with a deep, authoritative voice demanded. "What the hell? They are seriously rude. It is late and I didn't do anything wrong!" I whined. Fixing my hair before opening the door, I took my time to unlatch the lock. "Hi, come in!" I sweetly said, in an attempt to butter them up. Only two men walked in, although I knew that more were out there assessing my car. Immediately upon entering, the taller officer demanded "Are you Elizabeth Jeter?" "Yes sir." I replied, with the highest attempt of maturity that I could. "So, what

176

kind of drugs are you taking?" he immediately, and coldly asked. "I'm not…" I began. "Just cut the bullshit and tell me what you're on!" he interrupted. Tears began flooding from my eyes. I was so offended that he accused me of using drugs, which I had always stayed far away from. "I am not on any drugs! Drug test me RIGHT NOW!" I screamed at him. I must have been convincing, as he quickly changed his tone. "Ok, well I believe that you're not on drugs. Any person who is on drugs never offers to take a drug test." I nodded to affirm his statement. "I am Officer Michaels, and this is my partner, Officer Herald. Now, we need to ask you some questions. But if you lie to us, we'll know it, and you will go to jail right away. If you just tell us the truth, we can work with you. Okay?" he stated. "Yeah, of course. I'll be glad to tell you the truth" I said, gaining a small bit of confidence back.

Officer Michaels went to the back of the house to speak with my mother, and to inquire about Zoe and Chloe. Officer Herald would be the one to question me. We sat down on the stools near the kitchen breakfast area. He took out his notepad and began questioning me about the entire incident, start to finish. I recalled the events truthfully until it came to the demolition derby that I had initiated. What I didn't know was that I had already incriminated myself with a statement that I assumed to be innocent. "Where were Zoe and Chloe when you pulled into the parking lot to get the key?" he sympathetically asked, playing a definite "good cop" role. "Oh, they were sleeping in the back seat. They didn't wake up at all through all of the yelling, and I was so happy for that!" I idiotically replied. As we progressed into the interview, I answered my questions confidently with the innocent lie I had concocted to save my ass. "Elizabeth, I like you. But that is total bullshit. Just tell me the damn truth so we can get out of here and

177

resume our night!" He begged. He sensed my stubbornness. He knew that he had to get me to trust him, and get to my level, if I were to fess up to anything.

Tears began rolling down my face. I refused to admit that I was that stupid. I was more afraid to admit it to myself. "When Josh was between you and his car, did you want to run him over? Because he thought that you were going to kill him." He asked. "Of course not! I would never kill a person!" I said. I saw the look on his face. BINGO. He had all of the information that he needed. *Oh God. Dear God.* I prayed, silently. *Please don't let me go to jail. I'll never do anything bad ever again. Please, please, just one more chance!* I was not that kind of person. I didn't belong in jail. I was not a statistic. Everything would be fine, and like the officer promised, if I just told the truth, they would be moving on with their night. I didn't think that would include taking me for a ride in the back seat.

The taller officer came into the kitchen area and when Officer Herald gave him a nod he said to me, "Elizabeth, I need you to stand up." *Well, what the heck. Maybe it's just a sobriety test. Don't you get tackled to the ground when you go to jail?* I was wondering. I pounced up and flipped my hair, "Okay, can I help you?" I asked. He looked at me like I was a total retard. "Turn around, and place your hands behind your back." *Oh shit. This is not happening. This is one of those scare tactics you see in those Boot Camp shows. They are totally going to let me go. They just want to teach me a lesson.* I bargained. As I felt the heavy, metal cuffs tighten around my tiny wrists, the floodgates opened again. "You are being charged with felony vandalism, and felony child cruelty. You have the right to remain silent. Anything you say can and will be held against you in a court of law…" *Child cruelty!?*

178

Isn't that a bit extreme? What the hell! They were SLEEPNG!!! I screamed, inside my head. As the police officer finished reading me my rights, my mom looked at me helplessly. "It's going to be okay honey, just do what they say." she said, attempting to offer me reassurance. "But what about Chloe and Zoe!? My babies need me!" I said, sniffling between each heartbroken word. "They'll be fine, Lizzy. I'll take care of them." My mom promised, in a broken voice, also on the verge of tears. Helplessly, I walked ahead, with no shoes on, and no faith remaining in myself as a person, a daughter, and most painfully, a mother. I was not going down without a fight. I had an idea.

Coming this Spring

Playing With Fire

Book 2 of 4

The Elements of Life Series

Prologue

I sprint down the hallway as he's gripping the orange clay pot that held up an indoor tree; the tree had become all I had left to love and nurture. When I witnessed him angrily tear it out of the pot, the strong bamboo roots not standing a chance, I felt the fear of death pumping through my veins. Knowing my life depended on it, I leaped into the bathroom as I heard the whoosh of the heavy pot, racing past my head. The loud shatter, and storm of soil, brought a gasp to my soul. Locking the door behind me, I knew that if he wanted me dead, this frail trailer door would not save me. I opened the blinds to the tiny window above the toilet, hoping that my older neighbor might be home to hear my screams.

Silence overcame the weak trailer walls. The only sound I could recognize was the fast beat of my broken and empty heart. An overwhelming desire to surrender my life exhausted me, before unlocking the door and fearlessly walking into the hallway. Pale, with clenched fists, he was eerily silent. The gaze of Satan on his face pierced my conscious awareness of where I was and who I had become.

To support raising awareness to the teen pregnancy fad

www.facebook.com/keepourgirlsyoung

Or

www.confessionobsession.com

To sign up for updates on new publications, email
mcnewpublishing@gmail.com
with "updates" in the subject line.

If you enjoyed reading my story and would like to read more, please remember to rate this book. Ratings help to make my efforts possible in many ways!

Thank you for reliving my young, and insanely irresponsible, adolescent years with me. I hope that you were able to end this volume with a new understanding of what our young kids may be thinking, feeling, and facing in todays' world. Sometimes a quick smile just might be the only thing necessary to inspire a person to change.

Love Always,
Elizabeth

CPSIA information can be obtained at www.ICGtesting.com
Printed in the USA
LVOW07s2017220914

405274LV00033B/2037/P